FROM REPUBLIC TO EMPIRE:
The Roman Civil War 44B.C.-27B.C.

BY

W. W. TARN

AND

M. P. CHARLESWORTH

BARNES
&NOBLE
BOOKS
NEW YORK

CONTENTS

PREFACE

This book is a reprint of the first four chapters of volume x of the *Cambridge Ancient History* (published in 1934), on which the late Sir William Tarn and the late M. P. Charlesworth collaborated. Mr Charlesworth was responsible for the sections dealing with the west, that is the whole of chapter I, sections 3, 6 and 7 of chapter II, section 4 of chapter III, and sections 2 and 3 of chapter IV. Section 5 of chapter III was written by both authors in collaboration. The remaining sections are by Sir William Tarn.

The text has not been altered except to remove Latin quotations and references to source materials. Those who wish for fuller references should consult the *Cambridge Ancient History*.

The introduction is taken from chapter 17 of volume IX of the *Cambridge Ancient History* (pp. 738–40), by Professor Sir Frank Adcock. The publishers would like to thank Sir Frank for his help in the production of this book.

B.C.	ROME AND ITALY	WESTERN PROVINCES AND CLIENT-KINGDOMS
44	44 Assassination of Caesar (15 *March*). Return of Octavius. Antony given by the People five years' command in Cisalpine and Transalpine Gaul	
	43 The consuls Hirtius and Pansa killed at Mutina. Octavius declared consul (*Aug.*). Triumvirate of Antony, Octavian and Lepidus (*Nov.*). The proscription	43 Death of D. Brutus in Gaul
	42 Julius Caesar included among the gods of the State. Birth of Tiberius	42 Sextus Pompeius in control of Sicily. Battles of Philippi (*Oct.*). Suicide of Cassius and M. Brutus
40	40 L. Antonius surrenders Perusia to Octavian. Pact of Brundisium (*Oct.*)	40 Illyrian Parthini expelled from Macedonia by Censorinus
	39 Concordat of Misenum between Antony, Octavian and Sextus Pompeius (*Spring*)	39 Pollio recaptures Salonae. Agrippa campaigns in Gaul. Antony and Octavia winter in Athens
	38 Octavian marries Livia (*Jan.*)	38 Success of Sextus Pompeius against Octavian in the Straits of Messana
	37 Pact of Tarentum (*Spring*)	
	36 Lepidus ceases to be Triumvir. Tribunician right of sacrosanctity conferred on Octavian	36 Renewed offensive against Sextus Pompeius. Octavian defeated (*Aug.*). Pompeius defeated off Naulochus (*Sept.*)
35		35 Octavian campaigns against the Iapudes
		34 Octavian in Dalmatia
	33 Octavian consul II: Agrippa aedile	33 Death of Bocchus and lapse of all Mauretania to Rome
	32 Octavian defends his acts before the Senate. Octavia divorced by Antony. Antony's will published by Octavian	32/1 Antony and Cleopatra winter in Greece
	31 Octavian's third consulship followed by successive consulships to 23	31 Agrippa storms Methone in the Peloponnese; Octavian lands in Epirus. Battle of Actium (*Sept.*)
30	30 Tribunician power conferred on Octavian for life	30/28 Crassus in the Balkans
		30/29 Revolt of the Morini and Treveri
	29 Octavian's triple triumph (13–15 *Aug.*)	
	28 Census held by Octavian and Agrippa and *lectio senatus*	28 Messalla Corvinus wins successes in Aquitania
27	27 The Act of Settlement. Provincial *imperium* for ten years conferred on Octavian who is now called Augustus (*Jan.*). Triumph of Crassus (*July*). Division of provinces into senatorial and imperial	27/5 Augustus in Gaul and Spain

EASTERN PROVINCES AND CLIENT-KINGDOMS	LITERATURE, PHILOSOPHY AND ART	B.C.
	44 Cicero's *De officiis*. Cicero's first *Philippic* (2 *Sept.*). Cicero's third *Philippic* (20 *Dec.*)	44
	43 Death of Cicero. Birth of Ovid	
42 Ariarathes X succeeds to the throne of Cappadocia		
41 Antony in Asia Minor. He meets Cleopatra at Tarsus and visits Alexandria		
40 Death of Deiotarus, king of Galatia. Parthian invasion of Syria. Herod formally made king of Judaea	40 Virgil's Fourth *Eclogue*	40
39 Ventidius' victory over the Parthians		
38 Second victory of Ventidius and death of Pacorus at Gindarus. Antony captures Samosata		
37 Capture of Jerusalem by Herod and Sosius (*July*). Antony marries Cleopatra at Antioch. Antigonus executed (*Winter*). Ariarathes executed and succeeded by Archelaus in Cappadocia. Amyntas made king of Galatia. Polemo made king of Pontus	37/36 Varro's *De Re Rustica*	
36 Antony joins Canidius at Carana (*May*). Antony's failure at Phraaspa and retreat through Armenia		
35 Sextus Pompeius killed in Asia by Titius	35 Death of Sallust	35
34 Antony invades Armenia and captures Artavasdes. Antony celebrates a triumph at Alexandria followed by the 'Donations of Alexandria' (p. 101)	34/33 Building activity in Rome	
33 Antony again in Armenia (*Spring*) and legions left there until the autumn		
33/2 Antony and Cleopatra winter at Ephesus		
	32 Restoration of the Theatre of Pompey	
30 Phraates captures Media and restores Artaxes to the Armenian throne. Suicide of Antony. Octavian enters Alexandria. Suicide of Cleopatra		30
30/29 Cornelius Gallus crushes a revolt in the Thebaïd		
	29 Dedication of the Temple of Divus Julius	
	28 Dedication of the Temple of Apollo on the Palatine (9 *Oct.*). Mausoleum of Augustus begun	
	27 Death of Varro. The first Pantheon put up by Agrippa	27

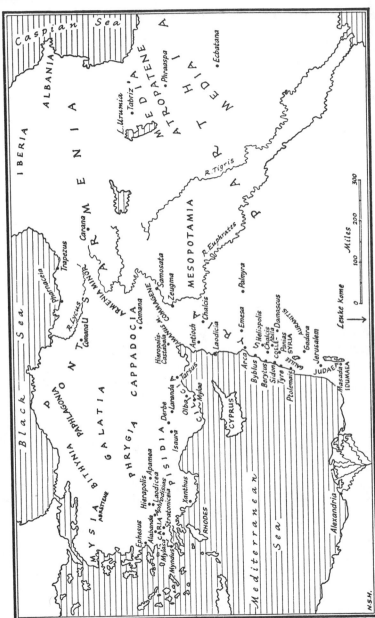

INTRODUCTION

On the evening before the Ides of March Caesar dined with
Lepidus, and as the guests sat at their wine someone asked
the question, 'What is the best death to die?' Caesar, who
was busy signing letters, said, 'A sudden one.' By noon
next day, despite dreams and omens, he sat in his chair in
the Senate House, surrounded by men he had cared for,
had promoted or had spared, and was struck down,
struggling, till he fell dead at the foot of Pompey's statue.

Caesar died the martyr of his own genius. No man has
ever been so determined to impose his will on others and no
man has been so gifted by nature for the achievement of his
purpose....But he reached power late, too late for patience.
The impulses of fifteen years of tremendous activity still
spurred him, but he was tiring....His health was breaking,
he had few friends and no one whom he would trust to help
him bear the burden as Octavian was to trust Agrippa.
For this reason he could not admit Time to his counsels,
nor share them with others. Thus he became, in a sense,
un-Roman in the last year of his life. There came the clash
between his genius and the Roman steady tradition, and in
the clash he was broken, with plans unachieved and plans
unmade.

He had shown the world the greatest of the Romans, but
he was not the creator of a new epoch. Whatever he might
have done, he had as yet neither destroyed the Republic
nor made the Principate. His life had set an example of
autocracy which his death converted into a warning. The
civil wars that followed the Ides of March prepared the
way for a statesman who was the heir to Caesar's name, the
avenger of Caesar's death—but no Caesar. The aristocracy

was almost destroyed, the legions became the servants of a man who was not a soldier first. The Roman world became ready to welcome the Empire that was peace. Caesar had done much for the State in his reforms, but he did Rome no greater service than by his death. The cruel years during which Octavian fought his way to undivided power were the last bloodletting of the body politic. A spark of Caesar glowed smokily in Antony and was extinguished: there remained Octavian.

I

THE AVENGING OF CAESAR

I. ANTONY IN POWER

The Ides of March, 44 B.C., closed in a night of fear and trembling; none knew what might happen. The panic-stricken senators had fled from the scene of the murder: Antony, the surviving consul, fortified himself in his house in fear of an attempt on his life also; Lepidus, the *magister equitum*, withdrew across the Tiber; even the exultant assassins, who had rushed out proclaiming Liberty, were forced to retire on to the Capitol by the hostile attitude of the people. Yet they held the key to the situation: all Rome waited to see what they would do; vigorous and decisive action on their part could effect much. In this expectation Cicero visited them; it was on his name that Brutus had called, as he held his dagger aloft, for that name stood for constitutional government. But though Brutus was determined there should be no more bloodshed, he was determined on nothing else; in the fond belief that the Republic would immediately be itself again, once Caesar was removed, neither he nor his fellow-conspirators had any plan of action or scheme for the future.

The first thing needful was to call the Senate and get the machinery of government in motion once more. During the day after the murder messengers passed between Antony and the assassins, and on 17 March the senators assembled at the summons of the consul in the temple of Tellus, which was conveniently near his house. An enthusiastic Republican like Tiberius Nero might propose rewards for the tyrant-slayers, others might clamour for the casting of Caesar's body into the Tiber, but more moderate counsels

soon prevailed, for Antony's speech revealed clearly the
unpleasant fact that the cancellation of Caesar's *acta* meant
that many of those present would have to forfeit their position and hopes of a career. Cicero used all his influence in
favour of a general amnesty, Munatius Plancus and others
supported him, and the illogical compromise was finally
reached that, while no inquiry should be held about the
murder, Caesar's will and *acta* (not only those already published, but also those projects which could be found among
his papers) should be confirmed, and a public funeral
granted to the body. After the meeting the conspirators
were invited by the Caesarians to dine with them and
relations were thus re-established.

But at a stroke the initiative had now passed to Antony,
and he was quick to take advantage of it. His early years
had revolved around the exuberant pleasures of an aristocratic life in the capital, amid love-affairs and debt and
rioting, followed by campaigns in the East wherein he had
distinguished himself. But Caesar's insight had appraised his
vigour and courage and found a use for him, and though for
some time he fell into disfavour, after the battle of Munda
he was received back and even chosen to ride next to Caesar
himself on the journey through Italy. He was the most
trusted of Caesar's lieutenants, colleague in the consulship
with Caesar himself, and likely enough (as he had hoped
and hinted) to be Caesar's heir and son. Hence his zeal for
the confirmation of the *acta* and will, and bitter must have
been his disappointment when the will was opened in his
house and he learnt that Caesar's great-nephew had been
preferred to him and that he was only mentioned among
the *heredes secundi*. But his opportunity had come now and
he meant to seize it; in the prime of life,[1] of proved bravery

---

[1] His birth falls in either 82 or 81 B.C.; his birthday was 14 January, as
recorded by the Verulae calendar.

and resourcefulness in action, a ready speaker, popular with the soldiery for his easy-going ways, splendidly impulsive and direct, he must have appeared the natural leader for the Caesarian party: what fate had yet to manifest was whether under this dashing exterior lay a unity of purpose or a controlling intelligence that might mark him out as a great statesman. For the moment the bankruptcy of counsel displayed by the conspirators gave him the very chance he needed; his first aim obviously was to conciliate the assassins and get them out of the way, to bind his fellow Caesarians to himself by tactful concessions, to satisfy the Senate by a semblance of constitutionality, and then to gain an important command for himself in some province near Italy. He had (with the consent of Calpurnia) already taken possession of all Caesar's papers and funds and during the next few weeks he worked with notable energy and success.

Each item on this programme was carried out smoothly. The news of Caesar's lavish benefactions to the Roman people had spread quickly,[1] and when on 20 March the procession escorting the body of the dictator filed into the Forum, amid all the pomp and moving ceremonial of a Roman funeral, the mob needed little rousing. As it listened to the recital of the honours heaped upon him and the oath that the whole Senate had taken to protect him, as it saw the toga in which he had been murdered, sympathy was soon excited and Antony had but to add a few words; a transport of fury against the assassins seized it, and fire and rioting broke out. Urged on by various leaders the populace soon became so formidable that within a month Brutus and Cassius found it prudent to leave the city.[2]

---

[1] The will was opened after the meeting of the Senate on the 17th; Caesar had bequeathed his Transtiberine gardens and 300 sesterces per man to the citizens of Rome.

[2] The date would seem to lie between 9 April and 13 April.

Antony demonstrated his friendliness by procuring a decree allowing Brutus to be absent from the city for more than ten days, which was the legal limit for the urban praetor. To the Caesarians he was all favours: when Dolabella abruptly assumed the consulship (to which Caesar had intended him to succeed in his place) he made no objection, though a few months ago he had opposed it bitterly, and for Lepidus, who had already promised him his support on 16 March, he gained by an irregular election the coveted office of Pontifex maximus. Finally he won over the senators, who had been shocked at the consequences of the funeral, by a motion abolishing for ever the dictatorship, such as Sulla or Caesar had held, and by empowering Lepidus, who was on the point of setting out for his provinces of Old Gaul and Nearer Spain, to negotiate with young Sextus Pompeius, who was still at large with six legions in Spain; to Cicero too he wrote in the most amicable and flattering terms. As Decimus Brutus had left for his province of Gallia Cisalpina in early April, Antony was now free of the embarrassing presence of the conspirators, and could feel he had conciliated all; the Senate showed its gratification by decreeing the province of Macedonia to himself and that of Syria to Dolabella. But unfortunately Antony could not rest here; the possession of Caesar's papers gave him opportunities, too tempting to lose, of winning supporters and raking in money. Though he published much which was genuine (as, for instance, the drafts which were given the force of law by the Lex Antonia de actis confirmandis in June) or had been among Caesar's intentions, he invented more: Roman citizenship was bestowed on the Sicilians, Deiotarus given the kingdom of Armenia Minor, possible helpers smuggled into the Senate, privileges and exemptions sold, and a steady process of embezzlement of the treasure in the temple of Ops began.

But in the long run he must rely upon Caesar's veterans: he and Dolabella had carried a law assigning land to them, and towards the end of April, with his beard grown long in symbol of mourning for the murdered dictator, he left for Campania to supervise personally the work of allotment, and to assure himself of their fidelity. Some weeks before, Cleopatra, bereft of her protector, had left with her young son in flight for Egypt.

Within two months of the murder of Caesar his chief lieutenant had, by skilful manœuvring, gathered the State into his hands and rendered his opponents helpless. Cicero lamented that despotism still lived though the despot was dead, but he could do nothing. For a time he was consoled by news of the repressive measures taken by Dolabella against the enthusiastic mob, who, urged on by an adventurer Herophilus, had erected on the site of Caesar's pyre a pillar at which they made offerings, but it was small recompense for lack of freedom. But, as May was ending, the announcement that a claimant to Caesar's fortune, who might disturb his plans, had appeared in Rome impelled Antony to return to the city.

2. THE YOUNG OCTAVIUS[1]

The new arrival, C. Octavius, was for nearly sixty years to play a leading part in the history of Rome and of the world. Ancient writers, struck by the contrast between the alleged villainies of the early Octavius and the acknowledged beneficence of the later Augustus, elaborated the picture of a young man for whom no wickedness was too base but who, through sheer satiety, turned to mildness and wisdom: many moderns, rejecting the rhetoric but retaining the

---

[1] Octavian is referred to by his real name, Octavius, until his adoption (see p. 22).

contrast, postulate a change somewhere but leave it un-
explained. Yet such a conception violates the laws of
psychology and probability alike: anyone who would
understand the character and achievement of Augustus must
realize from the outset that most of the charges commonly
brought against his youth or early manhood—immorality,
cowardice, treachery—are based on no firmer foundation
than the accusations and polemic of his personal enemies
and are worthless.[1] This fact cannot be too strongly stressed
and once acknowledged it is not difficult for the historian to
discern, from careful and sympathetic study, how the boy
Octavius could develop into the future Augustus.

His father, C. Octavius, belonged to an old and respectable, but not distinguished, family from Velitrae; his
mother Atia, a niece of Julius Caesar, had borne to her
husband two children, the elder a girl, Octavia, and Octavius himself, whose birth fell on 23 September 63 B.C., in
the consulship of Cicero. Four years later the father died
and Atia, though she married L. Marcius Philippus, devoted
her time, like a Cornelia, to the education of her children.
Octavius was not strong constitutionally; time and
again he was attacked by serious illnesses, and his health
always needed careful nursing. From his mother he im-
bibed the veneration for the traditions and religion of
Rome that is so marked a trait in his character, and learnt
the glories of the clan to which she belonged. His teachers
were some of the most celebrated of the day, M. Epidius,
Apollodorus of Pergamum, and Arius of Alexandria; the
affection he felt for them may be gauged by the fact that
he gave his old *paedagogus* Sphaerus a public funeral and

---

[1] The charges against his youth and morals come from Sextus Pompeius,
Mark Antony and his brother Lucius: charges of cowardice, as e.g. at
Mutina, and repeated for Philippi, come from Mark Antony and are re-
futed by Cicero.

recognized later as just causes for freeing a slave devoted service as nurse or teacher. The promise he showed, his exceptional beauty and nobility of bearing, and a discretion and intelligence beyond his years, no less than the family connection, brought him to the notice of his great-uncle. From a boy the name and fame of Julius Caesar can never have been far from his thoughts, and he made him the pattern of his ambition, for it was Julius who introduced him to political life, allowing him at the age of twelve the honour of pronouncing the *laudatio* over his grandmother Julia (including as it would the past history and glory of the *gens Iulia*), and promoting him to a place in the pontifical college. Like any Roman boy brought up on the tradition of *pietas* and *gloria* he longed to accompany his great-uncle but his mother refused to let him go to Africa on the ground of his ill-health; still, he received the *dona militaria* and rode in the triumph of 46 B.C. Next year illness again almost prevented his going to Spain, but he joined Caesar after the culminating victory at Munda and came back with him to Italy. Greatness calls to greatness: it is idle to speculate what he may have learnt from Caesar even in that short period of association, but the impact of so tremendous a personality upon the lad must have been overwhelming: on the other side, too, it is noteworthy that Caesar (unknown to him) in September 45 had decided to make him his heir. In the late autumn Caesar sent him over to Apollonia, accompanied by friends such as M. Agrippa and Q. Salvidienus Rufus, to complete his studies and to pick up army life amid the officers and men of the legions in training there; the eighteen-year-old boy could look forward to having his taste of war at last in the coming Parthian campaigns.

Such had been his upbringing and career when on a late March evening came the terrific news that his great-uncle had been murdered, among the very senators who had sworn an oath to protect his life, by men whom he had spared, pardoned, and even promoted. All the ambitions and hopes of a delicate boy at the very moment when life seemed opening for him, all the love and admiration which had centred for so long in his great relative, were now suddenly fused by horror and pity into a white heat of fury against his murderers; everything bade him avenge his death, but so deep and strong was his passion that it called for deliberation, where a lesser passion would have rushed into action. He even rejected as untimely the suggestion of some officers that he should march on Rome at their head (for the men were ready), though he thanked them for their loyalty. Instead, with a few friends, uncertain how he would be greeted, he determined to come to Italy, and landed obscurely near Brundisium.

Now came the second shock. Welcomed by the garrison at Brundisium, he learnt for the first time that Caesar had left him heir to three-quarters of his estate and had adopted him as his son. He was already resolved to avenge the murder; the news that Caesar had thought him worthy of his name and (who could tell?) of his position gave the final edge to his resolution. To his mother, who tried to dissuade him from entering upon a perilous inheritance, he replied with Achilles' cry to Thetis when she too warned him of danger;[1] to all his elders' prudent cautionings he could only repeat that he dared not think himself unworthy of that name of which Caesar had thought him worthy. Henceforward he could not go back: the image of the murdered dictator was ever present to his mind; to avenge his death and then to complete his work became the sacred object of his life.

Yet in the pursuit of that object he was to meet many

---

[1] *Iliad*, XVIII, 98 ff.

obstacles: his own ill-health he overcame by the sheer courage of a will that refused to give in; against enemies or against those who (as he considered) would not further or who misunderstood his father's plans he was to struggle for some fifteen years, sometimes openly and in strength, sometimes with the weapon of weakness, deceit, but always with one overmastering motive and with the clear consciousness of work reserved for him. And that consciousness came to him early, a consolation in perplexity (as to many another great man): in mid-July, when, against opposition and backed only by a few, he was celebrating the Ludi Victoriae Caesaris, a comet appeared in the heavens: the populace took it as a proof of Caesar's final reception among the gods, and he naturally encouraged this belief; but with an inner joy he recognized it as a sign for himself and knew his manifest destiny.

Meanwhile to work. He sent agents to secure the funds that Caesar had deposited in Asia for the Parthian war. Near Naples, in mid-April, he met Cicero, who despite his mistrust was impressed by his modest bearing and flattered by his attentions: 'He is completely devoted to me,' he wrote to Atticus, though he agreed (perhaps with some malicious anticipation) that there was bound to be 'a terrible *fracas* between him and Antony'. As Octavius entered Rome, towards the end of April, a halo round the sun seemed to promise divine favour, and his advent was welcomed by veterans and populace alike, and by a few true friends of Caesar such as Matius, who found in him 'a young man of the highest promise and well worthy Caesar'. He was allowed to address the people, and in doing so made no secret of his claim to Caesar's name and Caesar's money or of his views about the assassins; as soon as Antony returned he lost no time in visiting him; in the gardens of Pompey he placed his claim before him and asked for his help, but found himself treated with patronizing contempt and rebuffed.

For to Antony Octavius' arrival was likely to prove an embarrassing factor; up to now, while he had been the obvious leader for all who were devoted to Caesar, his reasonable and tactful bearing had averted any serious division in the State.[1] But if he upheld the boy's claim, apart from the annoyance of having to surrender the great riches he had so easily acquired he would almost certainly offend Senate and 'Liberators', which was far from his intention; if he did not, the boy would win support from Caesar's friends and veterans, who might well ask why nothing had been done to avenge the murder. However intelligible his irritation, it betrayed him into a blunder which was to have far-reaching consequences; he was after all the person to whom Octavius would naturally turn for support, the trusted colleague and friend of Julius Caesar, and from the day that Octavius found himself set aside and despised he could never trust Antony fully again. Antony had allowed his resentment to cloud his judgement, when tact and forbearance might have achieved much; and the appearance of a rival so disturbed him that he determined to grasp at once the power and the provinces he desired. On 3 June a resolution of the people was passed giving him a provincial command for five years in Cisalpine and Transalpine Gaul, in exchange for Macedonia, though he was empowered to keep the Macedonian legions. At the same time his fellow-consul Dolabella received a similar command in Syria, and a commission which had been proposed in order to decide upon those unpublished intentions of Caesar which should become law was now revealed as consisting of the two consuls alone. In order to get rid on a

---

[1] It was not until October that Antony made any really hostile utterance against the 'Liberators'.

specious pretext of Brutus and Cassius, the senators were induced on 5 June to give them charge of the corn-supply from Asia and Sicily, and to assign provinces to them to be named at a later date.[1] Finally a new agrarian law was carried distributing all the available land in Italy to veterans and poor citizens. By these measures Antony fortified his position for the present and secured a large command near Italy for the future, and already P. Ventidius Bassus, a man of ignoble birth but a capable soldier, had begun raising recruits for him. He was irresistible, and Cicero in despair decided to leave Italy for the remainder of the year and return in 43 B.C. when Hirtius and Pansa would be consuls.

Octavius was not so easily disheartened, though he was meeting with nothing but opposition obviously inspired by Antony. First a tribunician veto held up the *lex curiata* which he needed to formalize his adoption, and then another prevented his displaying at the Ludi Cereales (which were held a month late) the golden chair and the diadem which had been granted to Caesar. Undaunted he paid such legacies as were due out of his own private funds, helped too, it is said, by his friends, and let slip no chance of demonstrating his *pietas* towards his father: he undertook personally the celebration (20–30 July) of the Ludi Victoriae Caesaris (for Thapsus) since the officials in charge of them dared not, and though Antony again would not permit him to exhibit the chair and diadem, the veterans and the people acclaimed him and were vexed at Antony. In return the consul denounced Octavius, but his soldiers remonstrated with him and in the end patched up a reconciliation between the two on the Capitol. But though Octavius treated Antony with all the respect due to a consul and an older man, the reconciliation was hollow, and more than a year was to pass before Antony realized how essential concord was.

[1] In July Crete was assigned to Brutus, and Cyrene to Cassius.

In the meantime Brutus and Cassius were busy collecting fleets before setting out, for there were rumours of pirates on the sea. Cicero had left Italy in disgust, but on the voyage contrary winds constrained him to put in at Leucopetra, and here the news of an attack made by L. Calpurnius Piso Caesoninus in the Senate on 1 August upon the conduct of Antony—and possibly the impression that dissension between Octavius and Antony might be encouraged—induced him to return. At Velia (17 August) on his way northwards he met Brutus, who announced he was leaving Italy to prevent any possibility of civil war, and a few days later Cassius with his fleet also set sail—not to the provinces allotted to them, but to Macedonia and Syria. Though Cicero reached Rome in time for the meeting of the Senate on 1 September, he did not dare attend for fear of coming into collision with Antony; the next day, in Antony's absence, he appeared and delivered the first of the series of speeches known as *Philippics*. It was temperate in tone, and subjected the consul's acts to a criticism that seems mild in comparison with later efforts, but it may be doubted whether Cicero would have adopted so definite an attitude unless he was already meditating support for Octavius; by November they were exchanging letters almost daily, and must have been in communication before.

Antony's position was now far less strong: true, he had had the satisfaction of registering several shrewd hits on Cicero's target, when he replied to him on 19 September, but his relations with Octavius had not improved. He made some effort to attract Caesarian sentiment by erecting on the Rostra a statue of Caesar with the legend PARENTI OPTIME MERITO, but when there occurred a vacancy in the tribunate for which Octavius supported a friend, and the rumour grew that Octavius wanted to be tribune himself, Antony not only pointed out the illegality of such a candidature but threatened he would use all his consular authority to prevent it. The reconciliation was breaking and early in October came a sensation; Antony put some of his bodyguard into custody at Suessa Aurunca and later had them executed on the ground that they had been tampered with. The suggestion that Octavius had tried to assassinate him was obvious. Whether there was any substance to this charge it is impossible to determine; so rash a step seems unlike the caution of Octavius, who must early have realized how important Antony's existence was to him, and Antony may himself have fabricated the whole story. But now, pretending his life was in danger, he determined on more decisive action; he would go to Brundisium to meet the legions he had recalled from Macedonia, extort what decrees he wanted from a subservient Senate, and occupy the provinces granted to him by the plebiscite of 3 June. Octavius was equal to the occasion; he too left Rome on a visit to his father's veterans and dispatched agents to Brundisium to work on the Macedonian legions by speeches and (a characteristic touch) by propaganda leaflets. In consequence Antony had a stormy time, for the troops asked why Caesar's assassins had not been punished, and contrasted the small bounty they had been offered with the generous sums Octavius had distributed to the veterans of Calatia and Casilinum; he was compelled to execute the leaders and promise further payments for the future, and so persuaded the men to march to Ariminum, while he himself advanced on Rome with the legion *Alaudae*.

It was high time, for Octavius had returned to Rome with three thousand loyal veterans raised without authorization and was openly inveighing against Antony. He was in constant touch with Cicero, asking his advice and urging him to come to Rome, but still Cicero hesitated.

He had spent the previous month fuming with resentment over Antony's attack and planning an elaborate and crushing reply, the famous *Second Philippic*; there is a certain irony in the reflection that while he was working feverishly on this tremendous piece of invective, he also found time to polish and complete his treatise 'On Friendship'. But between lingering distrust of Octavius and fear of possible violence from Antony he waited at Arpinum, and Octavius, hearing of Antony's approach, left Rome for Arretium, raising levies on his own account in Etruria as he progressed.

Events now began to move quickly. Shortly after mid-November Antony arrived in Rome with the intention of declaring Octavius a public enemy, but alarming news suddenly reached him that the *legio Martia* and the Fourth legion had gone over to his rival. There was no time to be lost: he hastily summoned the Senate for 28 November to an evening meeting (which was illegal), redistributed provinces among his supporters, and set off for Cisalpine Gaul to dislodge Decimus Brutus, whom he formally ordered to leave. Decimus replied with defiance, declaring that he would uphold the authority of Senate and People, and after these admirable sentiments shut himself into Mutina to stand siege there. However weak he may have felt, to submit tamely, without striking one blow, to being besieged was scarcely the way to inspirit his troops, and Antony completed the investment of the city before the year was out.

The departure of Antony from Rome, however, and his discomfiture by Octavius at last emboldened Cicero to emerge from his retirement. News began to be more cheering: Brutus had occupied Macedonia and Cassius was rumoured to have reached Syria; Lepidus had brought over Sextus Pompeius; from Gaul Munatius Plancus was replying to his letters in exemplary Latin, and best of all Octavius had made no objection to the assassin Casca—'the envious

Casca'—holding the office of tribune. The young man was 'sound', and Cicero arrived in Rome in time to attend a meeting of the Senate on 20 December, at which he delivered the *Third Philippic*. Both in this speech and in the following one to the populace he urged the instant prosecution of war with Antony and energetic support for Decimus in Mutina. For Octavius he had nothing but praise: the young man (whom he now addressed as 'Caesar' publicly for the first time) had, 'by his own initiative and exertions', raised forces and freed Rome from the domination of Antony; all honour to him and his gallant legions.

So the eventful year 44 drew to its close. The prospects for the Republicans were sensibly brighter, for the consuls for 43, Hirtius and Pansa, were not bound by their services under Caesar to be partisans of Antony, and Cicero could write to Decimus Brutus in a tone of encouragement and hope. The apathy and timidity of the past few years fell away from him, to be replaced by much of his former energy and something of his old ambition; it may be surmised that he was once more toying with an idea, that had always proved attractive, of acting as political mentor to a successful general, guiding the State by his counsels while it was defended by the strong arm of a soldier; he had failed with the great Pompey, might he not succeed with a younger man, whose deference to and admiration for him were so apparent? For the moment he was the centre, though not the chief, of the constitutional party, in close touch with Brutus and Cassius, writing to all (Lepidus and Plancus in Gaul, Pollio in Spain, or Cornificius in Africa) who would or could lend support. The issue was defined and clear—a contest between the claims of Antony and the State, but there was still one uncertain element, the mind of Octavius, who was playing his difficult hand with an adroitness that deceived all save a few shrewd observers.

3. MUTINA

On New Year's Day 43 B.C. the Senate gathered under the presidency of the new consuls to consider the situation. In spite of the insistence of Cicero, who saw clearly the importance of legalizing Octavius' position, members were not disposed to take the precipitate step of declaring Antony a public enemy, and after some days' debate a moderate motion by Fufius Calenus, that an embassy should be sent to Antony requiring him to withdraw and submit to the wishes of Senate and People, finally won approval. But Cicero carried his point that honours should be conferred both on Lepidus (for winning over Sextus Pompeius) and on Octavius, in whom he now professed complete confidence. 'I know the inmost secrets of his heart,' he assured his hearers, and claimed that Providence itself had intervened to produce this divine young man who had delivered them from the tyranny of Antony. The listening Senate decreed that Octavius should be given the rank of senator and should, together with the two consuls, join in command, as pro-praetor, of the force that was to be dispatched against Antony. February brought the return of the embassy with the news that their mission had been fruitless, for Antony, far from showing submission, had counter-claims to put forward, and the *senatus consultum ultimum* was formally passed. But Antony could still rely on his supporters at Rome to protract proceedings, and it was only after another proposal for an embassy had been mooted and quashed that Pansa marched out on 19 March, with four legions, to join colleagues, of whom Hirtius was at Claterna and Octavius at Forum Cornelii. In addition Antony had written to the two consuls protesting against their attitude, jeering at Octavius as 'a boy who owed everything to Caesar's name', and declaring that he him-

self was in understanding with both Lepidus and Plancus.
Evidence for this last assertion was soon seen in the arrival
of letters to Cicero from these two advocating negotiations
and peace, though publicly Plancus assured the Senate of
his unwavering loyalty.

During the early spring Brutus had begun to feel the
pinch of hunger in Mutina, and Hirtius and Octavius had
moved nearer. Warned of Pansa's approach, Antony determined to attack him before he could join his colleagues,
and marched up the Aemilian Way; but Hirtius had fore-
seen this move and had dispatched the *legio Martia* (which
had already suffered from Antony at Brundisium) and two
praetorian cohorts to aid his fellow consul. On 14 April
they came into conflict near the village of Forum Gallorum,
where Antony had laid an ambush. Pansa was badly
wounded, and Antony's troops carried the day and were
returning in victorious disorder when in their turn they
encountered Hirtius coming up in support, who routed
them. Octavius, who had been left to defend the Republican
camp, for his bravery in repelling an attack won the praise
of the veteran Hirtius; both of them were acclaimed as
Imperatores (15 April). Six days later Antony again offered
battle, but Octavius and Hirtius forced their way into his
camp, Brutus made a vigorous sally from Mutina itself,
and his only course was to retreat. Decimus, with his
famished troops, could not initiate a pursuit at once, and
even when he did he was misled by false information.
Meanwhile Antony, with one legion (*V Alaudae*) and the
ill-armed remnants of several others, made for Gaul and
Lepidus, and was joined by Ventidius Bassus and three
legions raised in Italy. A harassing march awaited him
over the Alps, but his courage was superior to all hardships,
and the real worth of the man showed itself here; by mid-
May he had reached Forum Julii. Though the Republicans

had triumphed, Hirtius had fallen in the moment of victory, Pansa was fatally stricken by his wound, and Octavius was left in possession of the field.

This unwelcome truth was not, however, immediately apparent to the senators: in their first reaction from fear they were prepared to be masterful. Antony was formally declared a public enemy, and all his opponents encouraged. At earlier meetings in March Cicero had succeeded in getting the position of Brutus in Macedonia legalized, though he had failed to secure a *maius imperium* for Cassius in Syria. But now the Senate was inspired to grant more: Brutus and Cassius were confirmed in their provinces and given a *maius imperium* over all governors in the East; Sextus Pompeius was summoned from Massilia to be put in charge of the fleet and of the coast of Italy; Decimus Brutus was actually given a triumph. To Octavius they were less generous: he was not allowed the *ovatio* that Cicero proposed, his own troops and those of the consuls were to be transferred to the sole command of Decimus, a commission of ten men to distribute bounties to the troops was appointed from which he was excluded, and the dispatches were addressed not to him but direct to the legionaries. The majority would doubtless have agreed with what Marcus Brutus wrote to Atticus, that there was a risk that the boy might become difficult to hold in check, and that Cicero's enthusiasm for him was a blunder.

Octavius naturally made no effort to pursue Antony; rather, through various channels he offered reconciliation. He would not surrender Pansa's legions to Decimus; the rest refused outright to serve under a leader whom they loathed for his treachery to Caesar. Thus the hopes of the Senate rested on Lepidus and his seven legions; Plancus on hearing of the news of Mutina promised to influence Lepidus in the right direction, but on reaching the Isère in early May he was greeted by confident dispatches from the man he had come to save, for Lepidus affirmed he was quite capable of dealing with Antony by himself. The next news was, naturally enough, that the soldiers of Antony and Lepidus had fraternized and that the two leaders had joined forces; Lepidus now dispatched a letter of pious resignation to the Senate. Such were the tidings that reached Decimus Brutus, toiling in pursuit, early in June, and all he could do was to join Plancus, who had retreated to Cularo. Lepidus was of course declared a public enemy and Cicero lamented his 'criminal folly' in letters to M. Brutus, through which a growing note of despondency sounds; nowhere could he discern honest selfless Republican patriotism, and Octavius would no longer listen to him.

It was true enough. In July a party of centurions entered the Senate-house to demand the consulship for their general. Octavius had eight legions to back him, he had played long enough with Cicero to prevent the Senate's taking action against him,[1] he was in touch with the other Caesarian leaders, and the time was ripe. Various reasons were advanced in ancient times for this change of attitude, but all—whether irritation at being referred to as a boy, or Pansa's death-bed exhortation, or a reputed witticism of Cicero's—are trivial when weighed against the calculation that in order to avenge his father's death and attain his honours Octavius was bound eventually to combine with Antony, but must meet him on equal terms. Last year Antony had been consul, this year it would be Octavius. The Senate temporized by offering a praetorship; he replied by marching on Rome and resistance collapsed.

---

[1] The story in Appian that Octavius negotiated with Cicero about the consulship and played on his vanity is not impossible, though full of Pollio's bias against Cicero: Brutus heard a rumour that Cicero had actually been elected.

Once assured that his mother and sister were safe and unharmed, and after distributing from the treasury the promised bounties to his troops, he could wait outside the city
till the elections were over. Some difficulties were felt, for
while one patrician magistrate remained the *auspicia* could
not return to the *patres*, but the praetor nominated two
proconsuls to hold the election, and on 19 August Octavius
and his uncle Q. Pedius were duly announced consuls. He
had reached the highest honour Rome could offer at an age
younger even than Pompey, and it was reported that at
his first taking of the auspices twelve vultures were seen, as
on the first *auspicium* of Romulus.[1] The *lex curiata* necessary
to confirm his adoption was at last passed; henceforward he
was Gaius Julius Caesar Octavianus. The full significance of
this—which Antony well realized—is obscured for modern
readers by the convention of describing him as Octavian,
a term only employed for him by his enemies or by those
who wished to be less than polite. To the Roman people
and to the legions he was now Caesar, and the name was
magical.[2] A Lex Pedia, which pronounced sentence of
outlawry upon all assassins after a form of trial had been
gone through, was passed as a signal for all Caesarians, and
with his army increased to eleven legions (three more
joined him in Rome) Octavian drew out of Rome for the
north. Pedius easily persuaded the Senate to revoke the
decrees against Antony and Lepidus.

The collapse of Republicanism in Italy was followed by
its collapse in the West. The danger of a possible collision
between the Caesarians in Gaul and the recently united

[1] This report was to be of great importance afterwards, when he was
hailed as the second founder of Rome. He was not yet augur, though he
certainly was by 41/40, as his coins show.

[2] Fear of the effect of this name occasioned the large gifts Brutus and
Cassius made to the Caesarian veterans in their army. A modern parallel
would be the usefulness of the name Napoleon to the rising Louis Napoleon.

forces of Plancus and Decimus Brutus was soon averted; Asinius Pollio, arriving from Spain with two legions, preferred to join Antony, and succeeded in bringing over Plancus as well. Decimus found himself deserted; his legions joined the victors; in a vain effort to reach Aquileia (? and Macedonia) he was captured by a Gaulish chief and put to death. It is easy to brand the vacillation of a Lepidus or Plancus or Pollio, but hard to descry what other course than joining Antony was feasible for them. All three were men of distinction who had served under Julius Caesar and owed their rank and provinces to him, and Plancus was certainly carrying out the great dictator's plans when he founded the colonies of Raurica and Lugdunum (Copia Felix Munatia) in his province.[1] The sacred name of the Republic meant little to those who had seen one man's genius supersede it, and in a period when none was secure realism sought the protection of big battalions; in addition it was highly doubtful whether their men would fight against their fellows in Antony's army, for one of the most remarkable features of these years is the 'war-weariness' of the troops and their constant efforts to secure conciliation.

The only menace now left was in the East, where the Republicans had succeeded beyond expectation. As Syria at the beginning of 44 B.C. was held by a Pompeian general Caecilius Bassus, Caesar had dispatched M. Crispus and Staius Murcus to deal with him and assigned the province of Asia to Trebonius, later one of his assassins. At the end of the year Dolabella set out to assume the government of Syria, and on his way through Asia killed Trebonius, who resisted him. But he was not to have peace, for Cassius, also bound for Syria, outstripped him travelling by sea, and won over not only the forces of the Pompeian Bassus

---

[1] The exact dating is doubtful: Raurica probably belongs to 44 B.C. and Lugdunum almost certainly to the autumn of 43 B.C.

but also those of the Caesarian Murcus, and at the same
time pounced on four legions which Cleopatra had sent
from Egypt to assist Dolabella. With a total of twelve legions
he had no difficulty in blockading Dolabella in Laodicea
and driving him to suicide. Urgent messages now reached
him from M. Brutus (aware of the issue at Mutina) to meet
him at Smyrna; he renounced a punitive expedition against
Cleopatra, and after extorting 700 talents from the Jews, enslaving the inhabitants of four towns, and setting up various
tyrants in the cities of Syria, he marched to join his colleague.

Brutus, too, had been fortunate. Landing at Athens he
was warmly received and young men such as M. Cicero or
M. Valerius Messalla Corvinus or Q. Horatius Flaccus
enrolled themselves under him in a transport of Republican
fervour. In Illyricum the legions of Vatinius went over to
him, and he managed to bring C. Antonius (who had tried
to occupy Macedonia, which the Senate had assigned to
him on 28 November and had ordered him on 20 December
to give up) to surrender. He was in continuous correspondence with Cicero, and his letters display a calm lenity
in curious contrast with Cicero's vehemence. He did not
wish to drive Antony to extremes, and he repeatedly
cautioned Cicero against the bestowal of excessive honours
on young Octavian, in which he foresaw danger. 'We
should be more keen on preventing the outbreak of a civil
war than on glutting our anger on the defeated,' was his
message, and he spared the life of Antony's brother Gaius,
though later he had to put him to death in reprisal for the
proscriptions. The news of Mutina heartened him con-
siderably, and during the campaigning season of 43 he not
only collected recruits from Asia but also received the submission of several Thracian chieftains, and conducted a
victorious expedition against the Bessi, for which he was
greeted by his soldiers as *Imperator*. With the booty gained

and the treasure contributed by the Thracian chiefs he
issued a series of coins proclaiming symbolically his action as
liberator of Rome, and in the autumn made his way into
Asia in order to collect a fleet, money and recruits, and meet
Cassius. By the end of the year the two Republican leaders
were at Smyrna and by this date the Caesarians too had
come to a meeting and agreement.

4. TRIUMVIRATE AND PROSCRIPTION

By the autumn of 43 B.C., when Octavian, leaving Pedius
in charge of Rome, marched out northwards, his object
must have been clear: however great the disparity of character and purpose among the Caesarian leaders, however
deep their mutual distrust, a year's experience had shown
that concord and a common policy were essential. Antony
and Lepidus had agreed to meet him; on the appointed day,
early in November, the three arrived at their rendezvous
near Bononia, accompanied by the officers of their staff,
such as Pollio and Ventidius, and by their troops,[1] and
(after elaborate precautions against treachery) conferred
together during two fateful days in full view of the soldiery
on a small island in the river Lavinius. The solution reached
amounted to a triple dictatorship, like the informal compact of 60 B.C., but whereas that had been a secret and
personal arrangement, this was to be public and statutory:
the three were to be appointed *tresviri reipublicae consti-
tuendae* for a long term of years, superior to all magistrates,
with power to make laws and to nominate magistrates and
governors. Each triumvir was also to have a province,
Antony taking Cisalpine and Transalpine Gaul, Lepidus
Old Gaul and all Spain, Octavian Africa, Sicily, and

---

[1] Antony and Lepidus brought seventeen legions with them; six were
left in Gaul under Cotyla. Octavian when he left Rome had eleven, and
the six new-levied legions of Decimus Brutus joined him on the way.

Sardinia; the division demonstrated Antony's predominance, for his possession of Cisalpine Gaul gave him the mastery of Italy and he left to his partners those lands which were most vulnerable by naval operations and in which Sextus Pompeius (deprived of his command by Octavian but still master of a fleet of more than 100 vessels) might cause trouble. In the meantime, while Antony and Octavian dealt with the Republican forces in the East, Lepidus was to govern Italy. But to carry out this programme funds would be needed, not only for the expenses of war, but also to meet the demands of the veterans. These were satisfied by the allotment of land from eighteen of the richest Italian towns (Capua, Beneventum, Rhegium, Vibo, Cremona, and Venusia were among the number), while in order to replenish their war-chest and to rid themselves of their enemies the three determined on a proscription. There should be no clemency such as had ruined Caesar: with unflinching logic and on approved 'Sullan' methods they would uproot all opposition.

Such were the terms of this unholy alliance, and after they had been communicated to the exultant troops, they were embodied in a written compact formally sealed and signed by the partners. Octavian now resigned his consulship in favour of Antony's legate, Ventidius Bassus, and was to receive Antony's step-daughter, Claudia, to wife;[1] Asinius Pollio was left in Transpadane Gaul to supervise the assignment of land there to the veterans and the three leaders marched on Rome, where a tribunician law of 27 November (the Lex Titia) gave them the legal status they desired for a term of a little over five years, till 31 December 38 B.C. The next day a table of 130 proscribed was posted in the city, with a preamble intended to justify

---

[1] She was his wife in name only, and Octavian sent her back to Fulvia in the wrangles preceding the Perusine War.

it; but a short preliminary list of the most important had already been issued, with no fine phrases, and the hunt was up. Nights and days of unendurable horror followed: the consul Pedius, who tried to allay the rising panic, died of sheer exhaustion; victims were cut down without mercy, for the rewards offered were large and payment prompt; terror ruled. Yet amid the wreck of civilized life there were still some whom rewards could not tempt or torture affright, slaves, sons and wives who dared greatly and whose heroism triumphed over all obstacles.

A few, who were guilty of great possessions, attracted the triumvirs' cupidity (though the prudent kindness of the wealthy Atticus to Fulvia had ensured his safety and Varro was exempted by the intervention of Fufius Calenus), but the majority of the proscribed belonged to the old aristocratic order, who had supported Pompey and the Senate, and notable among these was Pompey's surviving son, Sextus, who during the winter was able to lay hold upon some towns in Sicily. Proscribed himself he made every effort, by the dispatch of ships and men, to rescue the unfortunate fugitives and bring them safely out of Italy. Many escaped to him, others lay hidden till better days dawned, but even so the number of those murdered— three hundred senators and two thousand knights—was appalling. Only those who believe that the triumph of a party deprives its opponents of the rights not only of citizens but also of human beings will find phrases to defend the proscription. Rome may have ultimately profited, but a crime it remains, and none of the three triumvirs can escape responsibility. Indeed it is false to history and to psychology alike to exempt Octavian; granted he was young, yet in pursuit of an object to which both his duty to his murdered father and his own ambition pointed, there could be small room for pity; he may have tried to avoid

proscription at first, but he was the most ruthlessly logical
in carrying it out, once it had been determined.

Among the first to fall was Cicero: worn out by his
feverish exertions, his hopes and ideals crumbling around
him, he had left Rome in August. A few fragments of
letters to Octavian remain, the rest is silence. When the
news of his proscription reached him he meditated flight,
but the wintry weather and his own indecision drove him
back. The soldiers overtook him; his slaves were ready to
fight, but he forbade them; life had no more to offer, and
gazing firmly on his executioner he met the supreme
moment as a Roman should. There can be few whose
character has been more bitterly impugned or more warmly
defended, and fate ironically ordained that his own match-
less power of expression (as exemplified in his *Letters*)
should survive as the most relentless witness against him.
His native horror of bloodshed and of 'Sullan' cruelty,
his legal training, and his humanism as a scholar all gave
him a traditionalist standpoint, making him an admirer of
a stable constitution, where life could be lived in peace and
reasonableness, and of this he saw a pattern in the times of
Scipio Aemilianus before the Gracchi disturbed the State.
It was his peculiar misfortune to be thrust into an age when
all the arts of peace were powerless against brute ambition,
which left no choice to a reasoning and sensitive nature
save that between two evils. His vacillation was as much
the consequence of his time as of his temperament, for in a
real crisis he was no coward. In an age of apathy and cor-
ruption he could sympathize with the needs of the provincials and strive for better government: in his treatises his
insight so gauged the trend of politics that, as Nepos re-
marked (*c.* 30 B.C.), 'he foretold even the things which are
coming to pass now'. Yet it is not as consul or statesman
that he vindicates his claim to fame, but by the influence

that his speeches and writings exerted after him, so that (in the generous phrase of Julius Caesar) he 'advanced the boundaries of the Latin genius', and fashioned Latin into an enduring and universal speech.

5. PHILIPPI

An impressive act marked the opening of the year 42, for on 1 January the Senate recognized Julius Caesar as a god, and the triumvirs not only themselves swore to uphold his *acta* but also administered the oath to magistrates and Senate: henceforward Octavian, the young Caesar, was *divi filius*. The final arrangements for the coming campaign were made. The three triumvirs had at their disposal an army amounting to forty-three legions; while sufficient forces were left to guard the provinces, Lepidus with three of his legions was to maintain order in Italy; to Antony Lepidus lent four, to Octavian three, and it appears that the two mustered between them twenty-eight legions with which to face Brutus and Cassius.[1] Eight legions were sent on in advance under Decidius Saxa and Norbanus Flaccus, and during the early summer the rest were transported across the Adriatic. Difficulties, however, were many: the proscriptions not only brought hatred upon the three, but had actually failed to provide sufficient funds for the campaign, and the imposition of property taxation met with strenuous resistance. During the winter Sextus Pompeius gained control of Sicily and began to give trouble, but though he repulsed a small squadron sent against him under Salvidienus Rufus, his own inertia prevented him from joining the two Republican admirals, Staius Murcus and Domitius Ahenobarbus, in harassing the transport of the triumviral forces. Octavian fell ill and had to be left behind at

---

[1] Two, including the *legio Martia*, were being transported on the day of the first battle of Philippi.

Dyrrhachium, but Antony moved rapidly eastwards to link up with Saxa and Norbanus, who after taking up an advanced position had been outflanked by Brutus and Cassius and so had fallen back upon Amphipolis.

Since meeting at Smyrna the Republican leaders had dealt determinedly with all open or suspected enemies. Brutus had summoned the cities of Lycia to contribute to his war-chest. Xanthus, proud of its century-old independence, refused and when the legions encompassed it, sooner than surrender, men and women destroyed themselves and their city; the other cities gave in and paid. Cassius was more extortionate still: Laodicea had to pay for its resistance, Tarsus was fined 1500 talents; the Rhodians saw their temples and citizens robbed of 8000; upon the cities of Asia he imposed the burden of ten years' tribute. It was the last expiring act of old Republican brutality, but it supplied the sinews of war, and the two reached the Hellespont together in September, in command of nineteen legions whose fidelity was carefully reinforced by a share of the booty gained. They had sent Q. Labienus to ask for assistance from Orodes of Parthia—a mission that was to have far-reaching consequences—and now marched westwards, turning the flank of Saxa and Norbanus, towards Philippi. Prospects were good, for their fleets, under Murcus and Ahenobarbus, commanded the sea and had their base at Neapolis; winter was approaching and if an engagement could be postponed hunger might work havoc among the Caesarians. But it was not to be: though the Republicans had the better ground, though the two armies were approximately equal in numbers,[1] the Caesarians possessed in

[1] Antony left one legion, under Pinarius, at Amphipolis; Appian says each side had nineteen legions, but two out of the Republican total were serving with the fleets of Murcus and Ahenobarbus, and six of the Caesarian were presumably guarding communications or on other duties.

Antony the most vigorous and resourceful general of the time, and now that Octavian, despite his illness, had joined the camp they had a living reminder of the name and cause for which they fought. Against this personal element the Republicans could offer nothing.

Brutus and Cassius had pitched their camp to the west of Philippi, on either side of the *via Egnatia* and in easy communication with their fleet at Neapolis. A large marsh lay to the south, a defence against outflanking of their camps and a barrier to any enemy who tried to cut their communications. Antony saw that the only way to foil the waiting tactics of the Republicans was to pierce this barrier, and started building a causeway across. When Cassius replied with counter-works Antony organized a simultaneous attack here and on the camp of Cassius. His dash and courage carried all before him, the troops of Cassius were routed and his camp plundered. In the dust and confusion Cassius, ignorant that Brutus' troops had rushed into battle unordered and actually stormed the camp of Octavian, chagrined at defeat and despairing of the future, committed suicide. It was a heavy loss to the Republican cause, for Cassius was a better disciplinarian and more experienced general than his colleague, who found it difficult to hold his troops in check, and now, fearing the effect of a public burial on his men, dispatched the body to Thasos. For the present he moved into Cassius' camp and carried on the uninspiring policy of inaction.

The only course for the Caesarians was to cut off Brutus' supplies; their own were running low, and winter was beginning. Propaganda leaflets were thrown into Brutus' camp, which induced some to desert, and taunts and abuse were hurled at the Republicans; men and officers alike chafed under inaction, and at last Brutus, against his better judgement, perhaps afraid that his lines would be cut, perhaps mistrustful of the continuing loyalty of his men (to whom it is said he had promised the plunder of Thessalonica), late on the afternoon of 23 October led his legions out to accept the challenge. Octavian's troops played their part manfully and finally turned the Republicans to rout, Antony carried on the pursuit with brilliance, and night brought complete victory. But Octavian was still so weak in health that he handed over the guarding of the camp to Norbanus. Some of the leading Republicans committed suicide, some fled to join the fleet, a few obtained pardon; the troops, naturally enough, enlisted under the Caesarian generals.

Escorted and defended by a few faithful companions Brutus had escaped towards the hills, only to realize as the night wore on the hopelessness of further resistance; crying out, like some ancient Hildebrand, upon that righteousness which he had followed so unswervingly and which had at last left him destitute, he fell upon his sword. So passed away 'the noblest Roman of them all', the last representative of the aristocratic tradition, and with him died the Republican spirit, for henceforward men fought for a leader. His is one of the most famous figures in antiquity, yet the fame seems factitious and the figure has suffered strange distortions. To the oppressed and to revolutionaries he has seemed the ideal combination of patriot and philosopher, his name one 'before which tyrants tremble'; modern critics, emphasizing his dourness of manner, his bluntness of speech, and that superior expression which Cicero noted, heap scorn on *virtus* that could prey on provincials and kill a benefactor for the sake of principle. All this is beside the mark, for Brutus was a more ordinary man and no unfair specimen of the late Republican senator; what held admiration in antiquity was his steadfast adherence to a creed (however narrow) and his intense earnestness of purpose.

It is to his credit too that the murder of Caesar did not degenerate into a massacre of Caesarians; he would willingly have spared C. Antonius, and throughout he remained true to the principle he had enunciated to Atticus of unconditional warfare against extraordinary commands, tyranny, and all 'power which would place itself above the laws'. But firmness of character and loyalty to an ideal, however admirable in themselves, are not sufficient guides through changing political conditions, unless based upon an equipment of intellect, and intellectually Brutus was in no way superior to his fellow nobles. When all is said, his was a creed of negative principles, lacking any trace of constructive policy to meet the needs of the time, ineffectual too against those who fought for a person and a memory.

6. PERUSIA AND AFTER

Philippi finally shattered Republican hopes: Murcus and Ahenobarbus might gather in the irreconcilables and depart, the one to offer his services to Sextus, the other to maintain himself in the Adriatic with seventy ships and two legions, but there was no party and no leader of the prestige of Brutus left. Caesar's murder was avenged; forty years later the inauguration of the temple of Mars Ultor fulfilled Octavian's vow before the battle. But much remained to be done: the two immediately urgent problems were to bring the East into order again and to deal with the great mass of men who were or had been under arms. A start was made by planting a colony at Philippi and by disbanding all but eleven legions, and of these eleven at least two were composed of Brutus' and Cassius' old troops. For the future the two partners agreed to a division of duties and provinces, witnessed by a signed compact of which each kept a copy. The division showed that Antony was still the predominant partner: while Octavian had been ill and carried about the camp in a litter Antony's courage and resource had won both battles. The prestige was his and he could impose his will. But Octavian held second place, for Lepidus was rumoured to be in negotiation with Sextus and, until he could clear himself, was to receive no provinces or troops. In the new allotment Antony took the two Gauls,[1] together with the more important task of settling the East and of collecting the money which was required for the settlement of the disbanded troops; ultimately, he meant to carry out Caesar's plan of attacking Parthia. Octavian received Spain, Sardinia and Africa; this last on condition that he would pass it over to Lepidus if he proved satisfactory; we may assume that Lepidus would also receive back the seven legions that he had lent to the other two (p. 38 n. 1).[2] In addition Octavian was to supervise all the assignation of land and also deal with Sextus. Italy was to be common ground.

Of the eleven legions left Antony's share was six, but he borrowed two more from Octavian, thus taking eight legions with 10,000 horse, and leaving three legions and 4000 horse with his colleague. He left six of his eight legions under L. Marcius Censorinus in Macedonia, as the Illyrian Parthini were threatening, and took two with him to Asia. In the two Gauls he already possessed large armies, eleven legions under Fufius Calenus, and thirteen divided between Ventidius Bassus, Pollio and Plancus, but he was going to lose touch with his generals there.

So the two triumvirs separated, Antony to the East, Octavian to the West; he was not fully recovered, and the

---

[1] That is, Old Gaul (later Narbonensis) and Gallia Comata, for, on the request of Octavian, Cisalpine Gaul was now left without a governor and became finally part of Italy.

[2] Presumably, had Lepidus failed to satisfy, Antony and Octavian would have taken *Africa vetus* and *Africa nova* respectively.

fatigues of a winter journey brought on a recurrence of his illness which nearly proved fatal, but somehow he reached Brundisium. Arrived in Italy he showed Antony's representatives the written compact and gained their consent. To safeguard his provinces he sent Salvidienus Rufus with six legions to Spain to replace C. Carrinas, while in Sardinia he had two. Africa had been held for the triumvirs by T. Sextius, a soldier of extraordinary resource, who had succeeded in routing Cornificius and all other Republican commanders; he now handed over to the successor sent by Octavian, T. Fuficius Fango, but apparently still remained in the province. Such were the resources with which Octavian faced his task.

It was no easy one: Sextus Pompeius was daily gaining strength from victims of the proscriptions or runaway slaves, and Murcus with his eighty ships brought a considerable accession to his fleet; the soldiers knew their power and were in dangerous mood; the veterans demanded immediate satisfaction. Evicted townsfolk or landowners raised every possible obstacle: hundreds of poor wretches driven from farm and home were drifting about Italy or emigrating in despair; some few, such as Virgil, found protection, but the remainder mingled with the other malcontents and only needed a leader. But, despite all, Octavian's faith in his mission was unshaken; he was beginning to feel his feet, and could already afford to pardon some of the proscribed, and he had friends upon whose loyalty he could depend to the last. Such were M. Agrippa, who had been with him at Apollonia and was soon to manifest his ability as general and administrator, and Cilnius Maecenas, a rich and cultivated Etruscan noble, whose diplomatic gifts and talents for negotiation were increasingly at the disposition of his friend; these two were to be of inestimable service to him. Important too was the fact that they were contemporaries of his, unfettered by inconvenient memories of the Republic, unafraid to tread new paths.

As the work of settlement went steadily on, friends of Antony began to realize that he had made a mistake in leaving the execution of it, and the resultant popularity with the veterans, entirely to Octavian. Lucius Antonius, the brother of the triumvir, who became consul in 41 and celebrated a triumph for victories over some Alpine tribes, first gave trouble; he claimed to be a Republican, and not only championed the cause of the evicted but attacked the triumvirate itself, and by so doing won considerable support. Fulvia, Antony's wife, was at length persuaded by a steward called Manius that her husband's interests were at stake, and the three joined in fierce opposition to Octavian. Lucius, pretending his life was endangered, collected a bodyguard from his brother's veterans, Asinius Pollio blocked Rufus' march westwards, and orders were sent to Bocchus, king of the Maurusii, to attack and detain the legions under Carrinas in Spain, and to T. Sextius to contest Africa with Fango. The leaders of the legions, in alarm, tried to effect a reconciliation at Teanum Sidicinum in the early autumn; the terms agreed on, as reported by Appian, are mysterious—including apparently the restoration of the consular power and an equal division between the two parties of the legions of Antony and the confiscated property—but they remained a dead letter from the start. The legionaries made a desperate last effort to bring the two parties together at Gabii; but Lucius, either through fear, or affecting to despise 'the hob-nailed Senate of soldiers', did not keep the appointment. There was nothing for it but to fight.

The only excuse to be urged for Lucius and Fulvia is that they honestly thought they were acting in Antony's interest; indeed Lucius assumed the name *Pietas* as a symbol of his loyalty. But Octavian was in a most delicate situation, for how could he be sure that the whole business might not be due to Antony's prompting? Both parties wrote to Antony, but winter made communication slow, the news did not reach him till spring, and in any event he could not oppose his colleague without overthrowing the pact to which he had set his seal after Philippi. The actual course of the war demands no long narration; Octavian sent a legion to Brundisium to guard against possible reinforcements from the East, recalled Rufus and his legions, entrusted another command to Agrippa, and placed Lepidus with two legions in charge of Rome—a charge where he signally failed, since he allowed Lucius to break into the city. Fulvia was tireless; she and Lucius had six legions of their own, she recruited two more which she gave to Plancus, she wrote for assistance to Bassus and Pollio; but the position of the three lieutenants of Antony was difficult, for no one knew what Antony really wanted, and Plancus succeeded in infecting the other two with much of his native caution.

Lucius, closely pursued by Rufus and Agrippa, flung himself into Perusia: the old town with its Etruscan walls crowning a hill 1500 feet high was impregnable by assault but all the more easy to blockade. Octavian promptly drew great lines of circumvallation round it, and detached some forces to watch the movements of the three legates of Antony; in the end they retired and left the town to its fate. That could not be long; the investment was close and hunger—*Perusina fames* became a byword—soon drove the besieged to desperation; Lucius vainly attempted to break out on New Year's Eve, some of his more notable supporters deserted, and by the end of February 40 B.C. he was forced to surrender. His excuses were bound to be accepted, for Octavian could not afford to offend Antony by harsh treatment of his brother; he was dismissed unharmed, his soldiers were pardoned. Pollio retired northwards, Bassus and Plancus towards Brundisium, and Agrippa succeeded in bringing over two of Plancus' legions; but no serious obstacle to escape was offered, and at Brundisium Plancus and Fulvia took ship for Athens.

Far different was the fortune of Perusia; the city was given up as plunder to the soldiery, stripped and burnt; the ordinary citizens were allowed to go free, but to the senators and to the remnant of Republicans taken there Octavian was pitiless, and the last traces of opposition were stamped out. An attempt at a slave insurrection in Campania, led by the ardent Republican Tiberius Claudius Nero, was soon crushed; with his wife Livia and son Tiberius he fled to Sicily, and Octavian by a strange irony expelled from Italy the woman who was to be his wife and the boy whom he was to choose as his successor.

But the twenty-two-year-old leader had other difficulties to face: uncertainty whether Antony would return as friend or enemy made it imperative to deal quickly with Sextus and Lepidus, for either, if unsatisfied, might combine with Antony against him. Calenus had not yet given up two legions in exchange for those Antony had borrowed after Philippi (p. 34), and Octavian therefore bent his steps towards Gaul. Opportunely enough Calenus died, his son was too young to be left in charge of the army there, and Octavian took control for the moment of the eleven legions. So large a force could only be given to a man whom he trusted implicitly, and so Salvidienus Rufus was placed in supreme charge of Gaul, though L. Antonius was made governor of Spain; in addition Octavian could now present Lepidus with the two provinces of Africa and six legions from Antony's Gallic army wherewith to control them.[1]

---

[1] After Philippi Octavian still owed three and Antony four legions to Lepidus (p. 29): it is possible that Octavian claimed that in giving Lepidus six

The acting governor of Africa, T. Sextius, who had succeeded in eliminating Fango, surrendered his four legions to the triumvir, and for the next few years Lepidus remained there inactive, though not without schemes of his own.[1]

There remained Sextus Pompeius; here Maecenas used his skill in negotiations of which the upshot was that Octavian married Scribonia, the sister of L. Scribonius Libo, whose daughter was the wife of Sextus. To modern eyes the connection seems remote enough, but such alliances were an accepted part of Roman political life, and this one might be taken as affording Octavian some hold upon Sextus. What Octavian could not know was that Sextus, equally anxious for security, had himself opened communications with Antony and offered his services. Antony was returning to Italy; the prestige of the victor at Philippi still counted for much; all would depend upon his attitude and will.

legions he was paying off not only his own debt (for he had already given Lepidus another two to defend Rome, p. 37), but also Antony's. Whether he had any authority (under the pact after Philippi) to act for Antony, and whether Antony acquiesced in Octavian's paying his debts for him or continued to claim these four legions of Calenus cannot be said; possibly at Brundisium the matter was left in abeyance and only settled at Tarentum (p. 68). But the whole question of Lepidus' legions is obscure: what happened to the three which he retained in Italy in 42 and to the two that Octavian gave him in 41 is simply unknown.

[1] The only information about Lepidus' governorship is too vague to warrant any precise statement, though it suggests some injury inflicted on the colonists of Carthage. He raised six legions more at least, for in 36 B.C. he started for Sicily with sixteen.

II

THE TRIUMVIRS

The true story of Antony and Cleopatra is largely lost. Something can be made of Antony down to 35, where Appian ceases; but of Cleopatra we know comparatively little until the last scenes in Alexandria, when Plutarch, heretofore hostile, begins to use the *Memoirs* of her physician Olympus. The surviving accounts of her in our late sources largely represent the victor's version; they freely pervert motives and reasons, and have incorporated much of the debris of an unscrupulous propaganda war. Contemporary evidence from the East is very scarce, but what exists hints at something so different from the Cleopatra of Roman tradition that, in the present writer's opinion, there is small chance of the usual portrait of her being true. But there is little to put in its place; the material does not exist. The excellence of Appian on the Civil Wars might lead one to regret the loss of his *Aegyptiaca*, which portrayed Cleopatra; but though Appian of Alexandria, who still referred to the Ptolemies as 'my kings', might have given a more sympathetic account, he would no longer have had Pollio behind him, and the *Aegyptiaca* might well therefore have been no better historically than the *Syriaca*.

Philippi showed that the Caesarian party was dominant in the State and Antony was the most powerful man in that party. In the written compact drawn up after the battle the prestige of the victory gave him first place and first choice. What that choice was has already been seen (p. 34); but though Italy was to be common ground and the settlement of the veterans a common task, Antony in taking the East made the mistake of allowing Rome to accustom itself to Octavian as ruler and the veterans to look to him as settler. Provided that he and Octavian did not come into conflict the East offered him certain advantages—science and administration, wealth and commerce (both somewhat impaired), potential sea-power; but in fact, though not on paper, he surrendered the most effective sources of man-power to Octavian. And whatever compacts might be made, there were already observers who saw that two men attempting to share the supreme power must ultimately fight for it.

But years were to pass before Antony should seek the supreme power for himself, and then not of his own initiative. He was born to be second, not first; as he had been with Caesar, so he was to be with Cleopatra and Octavian. Though he remained a blunt jovial soldier, the darling of his troops, whom he understood and cared for, he had some statesmanlike qualities; in politics at Rome since Caesar's murder he had shown rapidity of decision and resource, he could pick capable subordinates, and much of his ultimate organization of the East was to endure, though under another. But his nature was full of contradictions. Cruel enough when roused, he soon returned to his usual good nature; sometimes great in adversity, in prosperity he preferred luxury and amusement; straightforward and often loyal himself, he trusted others and was easily flattered and deceived. His worst trouble was women; they existed, he believed, for his pleasure, and they gave him ample reason for his belief. He boasted his likeness to Hercules, but his strange disharmonic face, too long between eyes and mouth, reflected the discontinuity of his life; outbursts of energy alternated with periods of self-indulgence, and he could not follow an unswerving course or lay solid foundations for what he sought to build. For though he desired power, it was largely for the sake of pleasure; hence he himself might have been content with half the world, had he not been caught between two stronger natures.

He landed at Ephesus, where the people welcomed him as a new Dionysus; Roman governors had long been worshipped in Asia, and the Ephesians were only trying to please their new ruler and expressing the hope that he would be as beneficent as the god. The greeting did not affect Antony's own position or make him divine, but it chimed with his mood; he wished to be accepted in Asia as a philhellene and man of culture, and he rewarded Ephesus and some other cities which had suffered at Cassius' hands. Athens received Aegina and some small islands; Rhodes got Andros, Naxos, Tenos and Myndus; Lycia was freed from taxation and invited to restore Xanthus; Laodicea and Tarsus were made free cities and Tarsus was presented with a gymnasium. He summoned delegates from the cities to Ephesus: they represented the Diet (*koinon*) of Asia, model for many other Diets, but whether Antony now founded it or whether it already existed is uncertain; certainly its function as a vehicle of the official religion dates from Augustus. But the delegates found him anything but beneficent; as he told them, he had to have money, and after praising the generosity of the Roman (i.e. Seleucid) system of taking a tenth of the harvest (which made the Government true partners with the peasantry, sharing losses) as against the Attalid system of a fixed payment, he ended with a brusque demand for the same sum as they had paid to Cassius, ten years' taxes down. The orator Hybreas of Mylasa had the courage to voice the general despair, and Antony reduced the demand to nine years' taxes, to be paid in two years; probably he never got so much, for Cassius had plundered well. After leaving Ephesus he made the usual governor's tour of Asia Minor, holding courts in the chief cities. His judgements were equitable enough, though cities and dynasts were alike called upon for money; he was, however, slack with his followers, who plundered freely, and what money he did get he sometimes, in his easy fashion, gave away. But he had realized the weakness of the triumvirs at sea, and he used part of the money to build 200 ships.

In Bithynia he met Herod. Hyrcanus, the High Priest governing Judaea, had sent to Ephesus to ask for the return of Cassius' Jewish prisoners, which was granted. Emboldened by this, Hyrcanus—or rather the Jews, for he was a cipher—sent again to Antony in Bithynia to accuse Herod, the son of Hyrcanus' dead Idumaean vizier Antipater, of aiming at sole power, and Herod came to defend himself. He made on Antony an impression of strength and usefulness which was never to fade, and the complaints against him were dismissed.

As regards the client-kings, Antony's policy was to make no change till he learnt better how things stood; in a peaceful age this would have been sensible, but after the recent troubles drastic reorganization was needed, and his policy gives an unfortunate impression of laziness. These subject-allies were important to Rome, for in return for the title of king and a free hand in internal matters they guarded the frontier or bridled the local hill-tribes, sparing Roman officials and Roman lives. Their armies were at Rome's disposal, they often paid tribute, and Rome could remove them at pleasure; but it was fixed Roman custom that, if one was removed, the crown was given to another member of the royal house. When one died, his successor had to be approved by Rome. The two important client-states in Asia Minor at this time were Galatia and Cappadocia.

Galatia, besides the country properly so called, included inner Paphlagonia and the eastern part of what had once been the kingdom of Pontus, the country about Pharnaceia and Trapezus; while the kings of Cappadocia also ruled Armenia Minor, which made them responsible for the safety of the frontier along the Upper Euphrates. The king of Galatia, the old Deiotarus, had sent his troops to Cassius under his secretary Amyntas; but Amyntas had gone over to Antony at Philippi in time, and Deiotarus kept his kingdom. But on his death in 40 Antony divided it; Deiotarus' grandson Castor succeeded to Galatia proper, while another grandson, Deiotarus Philadelphus, received Paphlagonia; Galatian Pontus Antony gave to Darius, a grandson of Mithridates Eupator. In Cappadocia Ariarathes X had succeeded in 42, but the line of priest-kings in Comana had long been pretenders to the crown. Comana was at present occupied by a young man, Archelaus (Sisines), grandson of the Archelaus who for a moment had been king of Egypt, together with his mother Glaphyra, whom Greek cities called queen. Whether Antony had an intrigue with Glaphyra or not (the evidence is poor), it did not affect his policy, for he confirmed Ariarathes on the throne; Appian's story that he encouraged Archelaus without removing Ariarathes, i.e. staged a civil war in Cappadocia with Parthia threatening, is impossible.

But there was a client-queen of Rome[1] who stood on a different footing from these petty rulers, Cleopatra VII of Egypt. Antony summoned her to Cilicia to answer the charge that she had aided Cassius; and in the late summer of 41 he was at Tarsus, awaiting her coming.

---

[1] Client-queen in fact; but whether in law Egypt was *in fide Populi Romani* may be doubtful.

2. ANTONY AND CLEOPATRA

Cleopatra was now 29, the age, says Plutarch, at which the Graeco-Macedonian woman was at her best, in both mind and body. By descent half Macedonian and (apparently) half Greek,[1] with a slight tinge of the Iranian, she was by instinct, training, and pride of race a Macedonian princess; Romans called her an Egyptian simply as a term of abuse, like Dago, for she had no Egyptian blood. She was not especially beautiful, but she had a wonderful voice and the seductiveness which attracts men, and she was intensely alive, tireless and quite fearless; even her wretched coin-portraits have occasionally preserved traces of the eager vitality of her face. Apart from her attractions, she was highly educated, interested in literary studies, conversant with many languages, and a skilled organizer and woman of business. Brought up at a corrupt Court, she knew no conventions and few scruples; the moral code had little meaning to her; she was her own law. But she was to be a loyal wife to Antony, though certainly she did not love him; perhaps she never loved any man; her two love-affairs were undertaken quite deliberately, with the same purpose as all her actions. For the key-note of her character was not sex at all,[2] but ambition—an ambition surpassing that of any other princess of her ambitious Macedonian race; and the essence of her nature was the

[1] The facts of Lathyrus' life show that his mistress, Cleopatra's grandmother, must have been a Greek from Syria; one cannot therefore absolutely exclude the possibility that Cleopatra had a little Syrian blood, though it is unlikely.

[2] To bring sexual accusations against those you disliked (see p. 122) had been common form for three centuries. As there is no trustworthy instance of any princess of the blood royal in any Macedonian dynasty ever having a lover (doubtless from pride), it is obvious that there was some over-mastering reason, other than sex, for Cleopatra's relations with Caesar and Antony.

combination of the charm of a woman with the brain of a man, both remorselessly bent to the pursuit of that one object, power.

The belief that she was unpopular in Egypt is unfounded. She was unpopular with the faction in the capital which had supported her sister Arsinoe, and probably unpopular with some Alexandrian Jews (not with all Jews), perhaps because they, as non-citizens, had once been excluded by her, as they were later by Germanicus, from a distribution of corn to citizens of Alexandria during a famine. But the evil spoken of her by the Jewish Josephus is largely taken from Nicolaus, who after her fall had gone over to her enemy Herod, and only represents what was current at Herod's court. Outside Alexandria she was certainly popular in Egypt, especially with the native Egyptians. From 216 to 86 native risings against the dynasty, centred in Upper Egypt, had been endemic; not only were there none in her reign, but at the end Egypt offered to rise *for* her, and, though she forbade it, Upper Egypt rose against the Romans as soon as she was dead. In her relations with the native Egyptians she seems to stand close to Alexander; and in some way she had won their confidence. One reason may have been that she could speak to them in their own language, a thing unique among monarchs of Macedonian blood; but much more important, probably, was her sympathetic attitude towards the native religion, which had laid its spell upon her (p. 85). Alexander had sacrificed to Apis, but she went further: she began her reign by going to Upper Egypt, to the very centre of the old disaffection, and in person, at the head of her fleet and of the burghers and priests of Thebes and Hermonthis, escorted a new Buchis bull to his home; for Buchis, the sacred bull of Hermonthis, was the manifestation of the Sun-god Re, whose daughter she was. At Hermonthis she built a temple

and her figure appears as the goddess Hathor in the temple
at Dendera.

These facts amply disprove Dio's story that she acquired
her wealth by plundering native temples. Indeed in the
first century A.D. it was believed that she was skilled in
alchemy and could make gold, having been taught the
sacred mystery of the philosopher's stone by a 'philosopher'
named Comarius; the illustrations to her recipe for making
gold still survive. The truth is that she possessed a great
treasure accumulated by her predecessors, the famous
treasure of the Ptolemies. Her father may have diminished
it somewhat, but he had met most of his difficulties by de-
basing the coinage, a process she continued; she intended
that her treasure should serve other ends than the restoration of a sound currency. Later times ascribed to her the
authorship of a treatise, extracts from which survive, on
weights, measures, and coinage in Egypt. Modern statements that the two famines in her reign were caused by the
canals silting up through her neglect cannot be supported,
for famine in Egypt depended upon the Nile not rising above
the 'cubits of death',[1] and there had been a great famine
under Ptolemy III when presumably the canals were in
good order. No doubt the agricultural system had deterior-
ated under the later Ptolemies, and Augustus found it
advisable to clean out the canals; but one point of his
measures was the deepening of them, which made a rise
of 12 cubits at Memphis a full Nile as against the 14 of
Ptolemaic times. But though Cleopatra did not attempt to
restore the agricultural position to what it had been under
the earlier Ptolemies, there seems no reason to suppose that
she was negligent in her working of the system which she
actually inherited; for in 32 and 31 she not only fed Antony's

[1] Seneca says explicitly that the famine of 42 B.C. was due to a low Nile,
as does Pliny of the famine of 48 B.C.

great army and fleet (p. 125) but also presumably supplied the grain for his depots in Greece, which shows that Egypt was still producing a considerable surplus of corn. She put on her coinage the double cornucopiae of Arsinoe II, 'Lady of Abundance', and her one certain surviving rescript attests a care for agriculture, and relieves from unauthorized local taxation some Alexandrians engaged in that business.

Many things after her death show what Egypt, whether Greek or native, really felt for her. One man gave 2000 talents to ransom her statues from destruction. For a generation she remained 'the queen', whom there was no need to name; two generations later the Alexandrian grammarian Apion was championing her memory; her cult was still a living thing in the third century. Alone of Alexander's successors she became a legend, like Alexander himself, and besides her alchemy there were attributed to her for centuries many of the great works of the past—the building of the palace and the lighthouse, the construction of Alexander's Heptastadion, the creation of the canal which brought water into Alexandria. Even in the seventh century a Coptic bishop, John of Nikiu, said that none of the kings who preceded her wrought such deeds as she, and praised her as 'the most illustrious and wise among women', 'great in herself and in her achievements in courage and strength'. But it is not only in her legend, or in her policy towards the native Egyptians, that she recalls Alexander. Mystically daughter of Re as he had been mystically son of Ammon, near to the gods as he had been, with dreams of empire that matched his own, there burnt in her a spark of the fire from his own flaming spirit, perhaps the only one of all his heirs whom his fire had touched.

The Roman story that she drank to excess may be noticed here, as it doubtless originated in a misunderstanding of her ring. She wore a ring with a figure of the goddess

Drunkenness engraved on an amethyst, the stone of sobriety; and a contemporary epigram explains the contradiction to mean that on her hand Drunkenness herself had to be sober. This gives the meaning of the figure: it was that Sober Drunkenness, 'mother of virtue', which was to play such a part in Philo of Alexandria, and for long afterwards, as the expression of the Mystic Wisdom or divine Joy of Life. In origin it was connected, on the Greek side, with the 'drunkenness without wine' of the Bacchic women; and what the ring, which is called a 'sacred possession', presumably did signify was that Cleopatra, like Arsinoe II, was an initiate of Dionysus.

It is said that Antony, when in Egypt as Gabinius' lieutenant, had been attracted by her as a girl of fourteen; but since then she must have often seen him in Rome, and she thought she knew what manner of man he was. She intended now to make use of him. As to his personality she had no choice, for if she wanted power she could only get it through the Roman governor of the East, whoever he might be. Had Antony been a different character, we might have seen a different Cleopatra—perhaps the friend of philosophers,[1] perhaps the business woman who ran a wool-mill with her slave girls. As Antony loved pleasure, we see too much of the Cleopatra who, legend said, wrote a book on coiffures and cosmetics. But how far she really understood Antony's contradictory nature may be doubtful; it was four years before she acquired any real influence over him, though of course events in Italy hampered her. She knew what she wanted, and thought she knew what Antony wanted; that she gave him, casting her bread upon the waters; she found it indeed after many days—when it was, for her, too late.

[1] Philostratus, an Academician, and Nicolaus of Damascus, the Peripatetic, are known.

She had been in turn exile, client-queen, and potential mistress of the Roman world; she was now a client-queen again, but she did not mean to remain one. She came to Cilicia in response to Antony's summons, and sailed up the Cydnus to Tarsus, adorned as Aphrodite, in her golden barge; Shakespeare has drawn that wonderful picture once for all. She took the upper hand with Antony from the first; when he invited her to dinner she declined, and made him come to her—the judge to the accused. All the resources of Greek imagination were lavished on the description of her banquets; if true, she would have needed to bring half the transports in Egypt. With the actual charge she hardly troubled herself; she had not in fact helped Cassius, as she proved without difficulty; but she wanted Antony at Alexandria, and took the shortest way by becoming his mistress. To be the lover of a queen flattered his vanity; he was ready to give her what she asked, provided it was no trouble to himself. She had never forgiven her sister Arsinoe (who *had* favoured Cassius) for her attempt on the crown of Egypt; she asked Antony to put Arsinoe to death for her, and that he did, tearing her from sanctuary. The Ptolemies had long practised dynastic murder, and Cleopatra had seen her father murder her elder sister, herself a murderess; in this matter she ran true to type, and the Antony of the proscriptions had no objections to offer. He also at her request executed her former governor in Cyprus, Serapion, for aiding Cassius, and a man who pretended to be her dead brother, Ptolemy XII. Before she left Tarsus she had his promise to visit her at Alexandria.

Antony spent little time in Syria. He confirmed on their thrones the two principal dynasts, Ptolemaeus of Chalcis, who ruled all central Syria with Damascus, and Iamblichus of Emesa; but he expelled some petty tyrants, who fled to Parthia. The Jews again tried to get Herod removed, but

after consulting Hyrcanus he made Herod and his brother
Phasael tetrarchs. He imposed heavy contributions, against
which one city, Aradus, revolted, and he tried to get some
money by a cavalry raid upon Palmyra, but the Palmyrenes
had removed themselves and their belongings into Parthian
territory. He made Decidius Saxa governor of Syria, left
with him his two legions, composed of Cassius' men, and
hurried on to Alexandria, which he reached by winter.
Caesar had entered Alexandria as a Roman magistrate,
with the lictors before him; Antony entered without the
lictors as a private man, Cleopatra's guest. The queen had
achieved the first step; she was no longer a client-queen, but
by Antony's fiat an independent monarch.

They did spend the winter in extravagant festivities and
amusements, and Antony did become leader of some gilded
youths who called themselves 'The Inimitables', but ex-
aggeration has entered into the things they did, both at
Alexandria and later at Samos. For example, Cleopatra
did not drink a pearl dissolved in vinegar, for vinegar does
not dissolve pearls, and an acid that would destroy one,
had she known of such, would have destroyed her also.
What she was seeking was to make herself indispensable to
him, both to guarantee her existing rule and to pave the way
to something larger; she was his good comrade in all he did,
whether hunting or fishing, whether in the lecture room or
on the streets at night, though she did remind him that these
things were folly and that his true quarry was thrones and
empires. She probably suggested marriage, as she was ready
to marry him without parley in 37; doubtless she impressed
upon him the advantage to himself of controlling the wealth,
resources, and organization of Egypt. But beyond that she
could not go. Antony was not thinking of marriage; he was
enjoying himself, as a successful warrior might; she did not
even succeed in making herself indispensable. The two

things certain are that he did not fall in love with her and that he got no money from her treasury; she was keeping it for a definite purpose, but of that she naturally gave him no hint, for as yet he was loyal to his compact with Octavian.

That loyalty explains his attitude towards events in Italy. He had known in the autumn that his wife Fulvia and his brother Lucius were making trouble, and during that winter the Perusine War was fought (see above, p. 37); but he did not intervene. The theory that he let Fulvia attack Octavian, meaning to reap the benefit if she won, supposes a duplicity quite foreign to his character; the theory that he dared not face the troops in Italy without the money he ought to have collected for them overlooks the fact that he did face them empty-handed a few months later. In fact he knew nothing of the war;[1] his last advices from Italy before navigation closed were sent off just after the arrangement of Teanum, when all seemed settled. He did not seek further information, because Octavian had accepted the task of settling Italy, and to deal with any troubles which arose was not only his duty but his right; and with that right Antony did not propose to interfere. What drew him from Alexandria was the news, received in February or early March, that the Parthians had invaded Syria. He hurried north at once, and nearly four years were to pass before Cleopatra saw him again. She kept herself informed of his doings through an Egyptian astrologer in his train, whose business was to impress upon him, in carefully veiled language, that to get free play for his own lofty personality he must break loose from Octavian. Probably she believed, from the political position, that he would have to return to her; but the world had no reason to think so, and only saw in her another of his discarded mistresses. After he left she gave birth to twins, a boy and a girl.

[1] Appian proves that he first heard of it in the spring of 40.

Antony sailed to Tyre, learnt of the defection of Saxa's troops (p. 59), and went on to Asia Minor, collecting his fleet. Censorinus in Macedonia was facing an invasion of the Parthini, and there was nothing Antony could do till he got men from his western provinces, where he had twenty-four legions—eleven in Gaul under Fufius Calenus, seven in Cisalpine Gaul under Asinius Pollio, and six divided between Ventidius Bassus and L. Munatius Plancus, all seasoned troops except two legions of Plancus' force which had been newly raised by Fulvia. But in Asia Minor he heard of the Perusine War and Octavian's victory. Asia had to take its chance; he must return to Italy. He did not blame Octavian; he had been within his rights. He crossed to Athens, where he met Fulvia and Plancus, who had fled from Italy, and also envoys from Sextus Pompeius, seeking his alliance. He must, too, have heard that Pollio had reached the Po delta, while Ventidius was near Brundisium. Plancus had lost two legions to Agrippa and had fled, leaving his remaining troops to join Ventidius. Fulvia told Antony that he must ally himself with Sextus; but Antony merely overwhelmed her with bitter reproaches. She had been a masterful woman, ambitious, and no more moral than her world was; but she had been devoted to him and his interests as she understood them, and what *she* saw was that, while she had tried to make him master of the world, he had first failed to support her and had then reproached her for trying to serve him. Whatever her faults, Antony treated her brutally enough; he left her ill in Greece without a farewell, and, with nothing left to live for, she died. To Sextus' envoys he said that, if Octavian kept his compact with him, he would try to reconcile him with Sextus; but if he did not he would accept Sextus' alliance.

By the time he reached Corcyra Antony must have heard that Calenus was dead and that his inexperienced son had,

on Octavian's demand, handed over to him Calenus'
legions. It seemed to Antony that Octavian had broken
his compact with him; he had taken from him Gaul and
eleven legions, and that meant alliance with Sextus and
war. But Sextus was not the only sea-king. Pollio on
reaching the Adriatic coast had got into touch with Domitius Ahenobarbus, and now told Antony that Domitius
would join him; and Antony, who wished to show the
outlaw that he was trusted, fearlessly set out with only five
warships and met Domitius' whole fleet bearing down
upon him. There was a moment of tense anxiety, and
Plancus was terrified; then Domitius' flag came down and
he turned his galley broadside on to Antony's ram. They
went on to Brundisium together, to find the gates of the
town closed against them.

3. BRUNDISIUM AND MISENUM

In closing their gates against Antony and Domitius Ahenobarbus, which they did without Octavian's knowledge
or order, the townsmen of Brundisium had acted unfortunately, but their action was natural enough. Domitius
had been condemned by the Lex Pedia as one of Caesar's
murderers, he was technically an outlaw, and only the
previous year his fleet had attacked Brundisium and ravaged
its territory. Antony's reaction was equally natural. Convinced that this was Octavian's order, he immediately set
about blockading the town and sent forces up the coast to
seize strategic points such as Sipontum. At the same time
he passed the word to Sextus, and Sextus too began operations. He himself attacked Thurii and Consentia in South
Italy, while four of his legions easily overpowered Octavian's
smaller garrison in Sardinia. Octavian marched hastily
southwards and encamped opposite Antony; Agrippa res-

cued Sipontum, and Sextus was repulsed from Thurii; at Brundisium there was a deadlock. But though Antony, by a brilliant cavalry exploit near Hyria, showed that the name of the victor of Philippi could still inspire terror, Octavian had already won over the veterans he had settled: they did not wish to fight, for they intended to reconcile Antony to Octavian, but if Antony refused, fight they would.

Fortunately the deadlock did not continue long: the veterans on each side began to fraternize; the news of Fulvia's death at Sicyon, though it came as a shock to Antony, meant that one of the chief causes of war was gone; it was not too late to think of peace and L. Cocceius Nerva, a tactful and moderate man, went between the two leaders, eliciting their grievances and trying to ease them. All would be well could suspicion but be allayed. Antony suspected Octavian of intending to keep Gaul and Calenus' legions and of having deliberately shut him out of Italy; Octavian suspected that Antony had been behind the Perusine War and was now making common cause with outlaws such as Ahenobarbus and Sextus. Characteristically, Antony made the first gesture, for he told Sextus to return to Sicily and discreetly sent Domitius Ahenobarbus away to be governor of Bithynia. The soldiers chose two more envoys, Pollio on behalf of Antony and Maecenas to represent Octavian; negotiations went well, the two triumvirs embraced, the past was to be wiped out, and as a token of restored friendship Octavian gave his own sister Octavia to Antony in marriage.

Naturally a fresh partition of territory between the masters of the Roman world followed. Antony agreed that Lepidus should be undisturbed in Africa, but the rest of the Empire the two divided between them, Antony taking the East and Octavian the West; though the dividing line passed through Scodra in Dalmatia both were to have equal recruiting right in Italy. Like Julius Caesar they nominated consuls for some years in advance (p. 58), and so secured honours and commands for their chief supporters. Antony soon gave an earnest of his reconciliation; not only did he put Manius to death for his share in the Perusine War but he informed Octavian of a piece of unexpected treachery. Salvidienus Rufus had been Octavian's most trusted general and rewarded with the governorship of all Gaul. The possession of a large army apparently turned his head; he meditated revolt, but was imprudent enough to sound Antony, and Antony as in duty bound warned his partner. Salvidienus was hastily summoned to Rome on some plausible pretext, accused of treasonable designs before the Senate and condemned to death—the first of a long line of army commanders in the provinces to arouse suspicion and suffer the consequences. In his turn Octavian gave to Antony the remaining five legions of Calenus' army,[1] and recognized the agreement with Ahenobarbus, from whom the ban of outlawry was now formally removed. He could also point to the fact that Antony's brother Lucius was governor in Spain.

The pact of Brundisium, which can be dated securely to the first days of October 40 B.C., was greeted with an outburst of jubilation by soldiers and civilians alike which reveals how deep had been the dread of civil war; the cloud had rolled away, peace was secured. Of all that human excitement and hope, too soon to be dashed, one echo remains, for Virgil fashioned out of the joy of that moment the famous Fourth Eclogue. Some seven years before, he had greeted the rising hope of the young Octavius, a fellow

---

[1] Appian implies that Octavian handed over the whole army, but this is impossible. It is more reasonable to assume that he gave Antony simply the five legions that he still owed him from Calenus' army, that is, eleven legions *minus* the six given to Lepidus (p. 38).

pupil under Epidius; then had come civil war, a reign of
brute force, and eviction. Now in the union of the two
great houses he foresaw the end of faction and warring and
predicted the birth of a son who would bring back the age
of gold; with this return he could link the name of his
protector, Asinius Pollio, who had brought about the reconciliation and who in the last months of the year assumed
the consulship.

> teque adeo decus hoc aevi, te consule, inibit,
> Pollio, et incipient magni procedere menses.

But joy was short-lived, for the triumvirs had not sufficiently reckoned with Sextus who, feeling that Antony had
played him false and untroubled by the marriage-connec-
tion into which Octavian had recently entered, determined
to assert himself. The addition of Sardinia to Sicily gave
him two bases for harrying the Italian coast. A raid was
made on Etruria, and corn-supplies were threatened. Such
were the tidings that damped the festivities that had greeted
the marriage of Antony and Octavia in Rome and the *ovatio*
granted to the two leaders, and depression sharpened to ex-
asperation as the cost of living rose and the triumvirs, in
view of a war with Sextus, imposed fresh taxation, notably
on slaves and on inheritances. The passing of the Lex
Falcidia, which corrected some unfairnesses in the existing
laws as to testamentary disposition by guaranteeing the
heir at least a quarter of the estate, came opportunely
enough for the new taxes. But at the Ludi Plebeii in mid-
November the populace broke into open riot and could
only be repressed by the use of the soldiery. For the moment
obviously Sextus must be satisfied, and at last he had
achieved his aim; a first interview near Puteoli proved
abortive, for he claimed more than the triumvirs would
give, but in the spring of 39 B.C. a concordat was reached off

Misenum. In return for concessions made by Sextus, that he would keep the peace, give safe conduct to the corn-supply, and stop receiving runaways and planting garrisons in Italy, he was to be given a large command for the duration of the triumvirate: Octavian was to yield him Corsica, Sardinia and Sicily (most of which he possessed already), and Antony the Peloponnese; he was to receive substantial monetary compensation for his confiscated property, to be an augur (like the other two leaders), and to hold a future consulship.[1] In addition all exiles were to be free to return to Italy, and this provision restored to their homes and eventually to political life such notable men as Cn. Calpurnius Piso Frugi, Tib. Claudius Nero, L. Arruntius, M. Junius Silanus, C. Sentius Saturninus and the younger Cicero. The terms were signed, and the treaty deposited with the Vestal Virgins; to celebrate the pact dinners were given to which the three came with friendly looks and concealed daggers.

Sextus sailed off proudly to his province; Antony and Octavian returned to Rome, hailed on their journey as saviours and protectors, and with all their popularity regained. To gratify Octavian Antony now consented to be designated priest of the deified Julius, and both triumvirs made arrangements for the defence and pacification of their respective regions. The north and the west of Gaul had been disturbed recently and to fill the place of Salvidienus there was only one man whom Octavian trusted sufficiently, Agrippa; he was given the governorship of Gaul, while Cn. Domitius Calvinus, a stern disciplinarian of the old school, was sent to Spain to deal with an insurrection of the

[1] L. Cocceius Nerva, the peace-maker, was already consul, and among the arrangements for future years the most important were—Agrippa in 37, Sextus Pompeius in 35, Antony II (or his nominee) in 34, Octavian II in 33, and Domitius Ahenobarbus and C. Sosius (both Antony's men) in 32. Antony and Octavian were to be consuls for the third time in 31.

Cerretani.[1] Beyond the Adriatic the Illyrian Parthini had
been troublesome, and Antony dispatched Pollio against
them. Far more grave was the menace of the Parthian
invasion of Syria and Asia Minor; early in the year Ventidius Bassus was sent eastwards, and in the autumn Antony
himself with Octavia crossed the Adriatic to winter at
Athens. For about a year exhausted Italy enjoyed a respite
from war or rumours of war.

4. THE PARTHIAN INVASION

The Parthian invasion of Syria in 40 B.C. was much more
than a raid. Cassius had not disdained to seek Parthian
help, and at the time of Philippi one of his officers, Q. Labienus, son of Caesar's general, was at Orodes' court. Philippi
marooned Labienus in Parthia; but in the winter of 41,
with Asia Minor denuded of troops, only two disaffected
legions in Syria, and Antony in Alexandria, he persuaded
Orodes' brilliant son Pacorus that a real conquest of these
provinces was possible; probably the fugitive Palmyrenes,
good trade customers, added their voices. Labienus and
Pacorus entered Roman Syria very early in 40; Saxa was
defeated, Cassius' old troops going over to Labienus, and
Pacorus got his eagles. Saxa held out for a time in Apamea,
but it finally surrendered, as did Antioch, and he fled to
Cilicia where he was killed.

In Cilicia the allies separated, Labienus going west and
Pacorus south. Antony's neglect to reorganize the client-
kings now bore its fruit; hardly one stood by the triumvirs.
Ariarathes of Cappadocia and Antiochus I of Commagene

---

[1] Both he and Pollio had resigned their consulships before the end of the
year to make room for P. Canidius and Cn. Cornelius Balbus, probably by
1 December. The army of Gaul was far too important to leave for long
without a commander, and Agrippa also may have left before his year of
office as praetor was over.

were pro-Parthian, while Castor of Galatia made no attempt to stop Labienus, who moved rapidly westwards, enrolling men from the Taurus tribes. Cleon of Gordium, a brigand chief in Mysia, killed his emissaries; but no city closed its gates till he reached Laodicea-on-the-Lycus, which the orator Zeno and his son Polemo, soon to be famous, held against him. In Caria Hybreas tried to hold Mylasa, but it was taken and razed, though Hybreas escaped to rebuild it later. Alabanda was also taken, and only Stratoniceia and Aphrodisias resisted successfully. Zeus indeed saved Panamara by performing a miracle, but Hecate, less efficient, saw her sanctuary at Lagina violated. This half-hearted opposition did not mean that men remembered Cassius with favour; it was disgust with Roman misrule, by whomsoever exercised. The Parthians named Labienus 'the Parthian general', and he put the shameful title, *Parthicus Imperator*, on his coins.

Pacorus swept southwards through Syria. He could not take Tyre on its island; otherwise all Syria joined him, including Lysanias of Chalcis, who had just succeeded his father Ptolemaeus, and even Malchus of Nabataea was ready to be friendly. Pacorus perhaps was now joint king with his father and struck coins, which may point to an intention to hold Syria permanently. The Hasmonaean Antigonus (Mattathias), Aristobulus' son, pretender to the throne of Judaea, now offered Pacorus 1000 talents and 500 women—the families of his political opponents—to make him king. The Jews, who hated the rule of the Idumaeans, welcomed Antigonus, and a Parthian force entered Jerusalem and seated him on the throne. He cut off Hyrcanus' ears so that he could never again be High Priest and gave him to Pacorus, who left Syria and took him to Parthia; there Orodes treated him kindly and gave him a residence in Babylonia. Antigonus struck bilingual coins with 'King Antigonus' in Greek and in Hebrew 'Matta-thias the High Priest, the Commonwealth of the Jews'. For a century the Jews regarded the Parthians with affection as saviours, for they had delivered the people from Rome and her Idumaean friends. The tetrarchs, Herod and Phasael, held the castle till Phasael fell into the Parthians' hands and committed suicide; then with courage and skill Herod collected the threatened women, who included his mother and sister, Hyrcanus' widowed daughter Alexandra and her daughter Mariamme, his betrothed, and got them away to his fortress of Masada in Idumaea. He left his brother Joseph to hold it, which he did successfully, and, after being refused help by Malchus, took the road to Egypt. To Cleopatra he was just a young man struggling to uphold Antony's interests; she gave him a ship, and he sailed to Rome to find Antony. He was fortunate in arriving after the peace of Brundisium; Antony agreed with him that only he could maintain Rome's cause against Parthia, and interested Octavian, who remembered his father Anti-pater's services to Caesar. An obedient Senate made Herod king of Judaea. Thus the first breach in the Roman custom that a new client-king must be chosen from the old line was made by Antony and Octavian in concert. From that day, whatever Herod did to his subjects, he never faltered in loyalty to Antony. He now returned to Palestine, raised mercenaries, and attacked Antigonus.

The legions at Antony's disposal after the peace of Brundisium were six brought from Macedonia, seven under Pollio, four under Ventidius, two from Domitius (who was sent with them to Bithynia as governor), and five once under Calenus (see p. 38 n. 1). Antony's army down to 36 con-sisted of these twenty-four legions only,[1] no extravagant

---

[1] A new factor was introduced when Lepidus took over four legions from Sextius in Africa, which Antony claimed as his; possibly, therefore, at

force with which to safeguard the Balkan frontier, manage
the whole East, and conquer Parthia, and sufficient proof
that he was not aiming at the sole power. He had retained
10,000 cavalry after Philippi, largely Gauls and Spaniards;
how much more Ventidius and Pollio brought him cannot
be said. Besides the Parthians, he now had to deal seriously
with the Illyrian trouble. The Illyrian Parthini had invaded
Macedonia in 40 and been expelled by Censorinus, who
triumphed on 1 January 39. Antony now gave Pollio eleven
legions and sent him to Macedonia where he successfully
reduced the Parthini, retook Salonae, and celebrated his
triumph on 25 October 39 or 38. Antony then divided
Pollio's army, stationing four legions in Epirus and leaving
seven to guard Macedonia and Illyria. The other eleven
legions not with Pollio or Domitius he gave to Ventidius,
with a strong force of cavalry and slingers, and sent him
against the Parthians. He himself was urgently needed in
Italy, and with more than one campaign to watch he
naturally did not take the field himself. Either he or Ventidius had realized that the sling, with leaden bullets, would
outrange the Parthian bows; but what neither knew was
that there had been a change in Parthia's tactics and that
it was not the archers whom Ventidius would meet. Carrhae
had been won by the common man, trained and led by
a genius; the nobility had felt slighted—hence perhaps
Surenas' fall—and they were now going to show the Romans
what they could do themselves. It was a great stroke of luck
for Ventidius; no archers are mentioned in his campaigns,
and his battles show clearly that Pacorus was relying on
heavy cavalry, the cataphracts. Antony appointed Plancus
to be governor of the province of Asia when cleared.

Tarentum Antony claimed that Octavian, one way or another, did owe
him four legions, and Octavian, though not admitting the claim, agreed to
give four legions in exchange for ships (pp. 68, 74).

Our accounts of Ventidius' victories go back to a rhetorical panegyric written for his triumph by Sallust from material supplied by himself after Antony had cashiered him; and Antony's opponents glorified him at Antony's expense. He landed in Asia early in 39 and surprised Labienus, who evacuated Caria and fled to Cilicia with Ventidius' cavalry in pursuit. He fortified a camp on the Taurus slopes and summoned the Parthians, while Ventidius camped on rising ground and waited for his legions, who arrived first. The Parthians evacuated Syria, but were too confident merely to join Labienus, and attacked Ventidius by themselves. Their cataphracts charged the Roman camp up the hill and met the legions hand to hand; they were thrown down the hill in rout, and Ventidius discovered that at short range his slingers could penetrate their armour. He then attacked Labienus' camp. Labienus lost his nerve and fled, and was subsequently killed. The retreating Parthians stood at the Amanic Gates, and must have dismounted men to hold the pass; it was easily forced, the defenders fled across the Euphrates, and Ventidius had cleared Roman Asia as quickly as it had been overrun. Antony took the title of *Imperator* for the second time for the victories of Ventidius and Pollio, and Ventidius marched through Syria to dethrone Antigonus. But Antigonus bribed him, and he did nothing; he went into winter quarters with his army strung out from Judaea to Cappadocia, that country being a danger-point should Artavasdes of Armenia, Parthia's ally, enter the war.

The new Parthian tactics were obviously wrong; but Pacorus had not been with the army, which seemingly was not numerous, and did not recognize its defeat as decisive. Early in 38 he assembled a larger force; he may have brought every cataphract in Parthia. Ventidius, to gain time to collect his troops, skilfully let him hear that he was afraid he might cross the Euphrates, not at Zeugma, but to the south. Pacorus, perplexed and suspicious, apparently avoided both courses and made a detour to the north, crossing perhaps at Samosata. By the time he entered Cyrrhestice Ventidius was ready and had fortified a camp on rising ground near Mt Gindarus. Again the Parthian chivalry charged the camp, with the same result as before but with heavier loss, for Pacorus was killed and some of his men died fighting round his body; the main force escaped across the Euphrates. Ventidius became extraordinarily popular, for he was held to have avenged Carrhae; but the story that Gindarus was fought on the anniversary of that battle is probably an invention. Pacorus' death was a loss to Parthia, for he is highly praised, not only for energy and valour, but for his moderation and equity, which everywhere attracted much support. But, except for that, the defeat of Gindarus was Parthia's salvation; it taught her not to rely upon cataphracts against a Roman army.

5. ANTONY AND OCTAVIA

At the beginning of November 40 the seal had been set to the treaty of Brundisium by the marriage of Antony and Octavian's sister Octavia, Marcellus' widow, the pledge that the two sides were henceforth one. Fulvia's death had left Antony free, and though Octavia had not completed the obligatory ten months' mourning for her husband the Senate obediently gave her permission to re-marry. Through the murk of the civil wars Octavia shines like a star; in an age when every restraint was relaxed, and Roman virtues seemed likely to go down in a welter of licence and cruelty, no evil about her was ever even hinted by anybody. Beautiful and still young, highly cultured, the friend of the honoured philosophers Athenodorus (who dedicated a book to her) and Nestor, she preferred her home to politics; but she was a match for her brother in diplomacy, as she was to show at Tarentum by her quiet but conclusive handling of his accusations against Antony. Her gentleness and goodness, and her devoted obedience to her husband, sprang from strength, not from weakness; what she saw to be her duty, that, quite simply, she did. She made no complaint of Antony's treatment of her; she helped him as long as he would let her, and when the end came she took charge of his children by the rival who had ousted her and brought them up with her own, the crowning heroism of perhaps the loveliest nature which the ancient world can show.

Antony did not leave Italy till after the birth of Octavia's daughter, the elder Antonia, about August or September 39; then he and Octavia went to Athens, which for the next two years was his headquarters. The Senate had confirmed in advance his measures in the East, and the disaffection among the client-kings revealed by the Parthian invasion invited a complete reorganization. He made a partial one only. Labienus had got help from the Taurus peoples, and Antony took advantage of the breach made in Roman custom in Herod's case (p. 61) to pick out two good men who did not belong to any dynasty but who had given their proofs, Amyntas from Galatia, the former secretary of Deiotarus (p. 44), and Polemo of Laodicea (p. 60), and put them in authority over the tribes. Amyntas' kingdom was western Pisidia and Phrygia-toward-Pisidia. Polemo had his seat at Iconium and ruled Cilicia Tracheia, a wild country which had once been part of the Roman province of Cilicia but which was difficult to manage. Antony strengthened Tarcondimotus, a dynast in the unruly Amanus, by making him king, with his capital at Hieropolis Castabala; on his coins he called himself Philantonius. Cleon, the brigand chief who had defied Labienus, was confirmed in his rule of the Mysian Olympus. Aphrodisias received freedom and immunity from taxation; Antony's grant is remarkable as containing (in simple form) a most-favoured-nation clause, apparently its first appearance in history. He also raised his fleet to five squadrons of the line (300 ships), partly by incorporating Domitius' fleet; if it came to trouble, he did not mean to be weaker than Sextus. He made fleet-stations of Cephallenia and Zacynthus, convenient for keeping watch over Sicilian waters, and posted detachments there under Proculeius and C. Sosius, who acted as lords of their respective islands and struck coins; the coins of Antony's fleet-prefects of this period are notable for their naval symbolism. Either now or in 38 he brought to Asia the four legions from Epirus, leaving seven in Macedonia.

He spent the winter at Athens with Octavia in the enjoyment of a new sensation, the company of a virtuous woman. He became respectable; he dressed simply, went with his wife to philosophers' lectures and the public festivals, and served as gymnasiarch (minister for education); perhaps it was now that he projected a universal association of victors in the games. Athens gave Octavia many honours, and the Panathenaia of 38 bore the added name Antonieia. But, if more decorous, Antony was as self-indulgent at Athens as he had been at Alexandria; he put aside all business till the spring, though apparently he meant to conquer Armenia in 38 as the prelude to the invasion of Parthia. For his Eastern subjects he now assumed divinity like a Hellenistic king and proclaimed himself a New Dionysus, the god who had conquered Asia (p. 87). The story that he married Athene and exacted from the Athenians a million drachmae as her dower first appears in a rhetorical exercise and reads like a refurbishing of the story of the marriage of Antiochus IV with Atargatis; to 'woo Athene' was almost a proverb for the insolence of power.

Antony's plans for 38 were altered by a message from Octavian, who was having trouble with Sextus and asked Antony to be at Brundisium on a given day for a conference. Antony came, but Octavian did not; and Antony, naturally angry at what he considered an insult, went back again, after advising Octavian to keep his treaties. Pacorus' second invasion (p. 63) prevented further thought of the conquest of Armenia, and Gindarus was followed by a fresh complication. Some fugitive Parthians had taken refuge with Antiochus of Commagene, and Ventidius marched on Samosata; but Antiochus, in imitation of Antigonus, offered him 1000 talents to mark time, and the siege made no progress. This second scandal created an impossible position, and Antony was forced to supersede him and take command in person. Samosata surrendered to him, and he presumably removed Antiochus, who is not heard of again, and made his brother Mithridates king; and he took the title of *Imperator* for the third time, really for Gindarus. He sent Ventidius to Italy for the well-earned triumph which the people had voted him and of which he was too generous to deprive him in spite of his misdoings. Ventidius triumphed on 27 November 38 or 37 and is not heard of again; naturally Antony could not employ him, and as Octavian never did he probably died soon afterwards.

After Gindarus Ventidius had detached a force to help Herod; but Antigonus again bribed the Roman commander, and Herod, in despair of getting anything done, went himself to Antony, who was before Samosata. As soon as Samosata had surrendered, Antony put Sosius in command with strict orders to deal with Antigonus, and Sosius sent Herod on ahead with two legions, a rare instance of a foreigner commanding Roman troops. Herod defeated

Antigonus' men at Jericho and went on to besiege Jerusalem. When Sosius arrived the siege was energetically pressed by the entire Roman army. Jerusalem held out manfully, but was taken in July 37 B.C.; Herod prevented the desecration of the Temple and ransomed the town from pillage, saying that he wanted a kingdom, not a desert. Antigonus surrendered to Sosius, who subsequently took him to Antony; and Herod, who had married Mariamme, the last Hasmonaean princess, began his long reign as king of Judaea. Sosius commemorated his success by striking a coin with the figures of Antigonus and of Judaea as a captive woman. But some Jews at once revolted against Herod, and that winter (37) Antony executed Antigonus lest he should become a centre of disaffection.

After taking Samosata Antony returned to Athens and again spent the winter (38) with Octavia. He was still not fated to reduce Armenia, for Octavian, after his disaster at Cape Scyllaeum (p. 72), sent Maecenas to him with an urgent request for naval help. Antony's star was in the ascendant; three of his generals had recently celebrated or been granted triumphs, and that of Sosius was to come, while Octavian's campaign against Sextus in 38 had been a failure. Antony stood loyally by his colleague, and in the spring of 37 sailed to Tarentum with Octavia and his whole fleet, only to find that Octavian, who had built a new fleet during the winter, now intimated that he no longer required his help. What followed is related elsewhere (p. 73); Octavia prevented war, and the result was the treaty of Tarentum, under which Antony handed over to Octavian two complete squadrons—120 ships of the line and their 10 scouts—against Octavian's promise of four legions which Antony perhaps claimed that he owed already (pp. 38f., 61f.); Antony agreed because he was short of money and wished to get rid of the upkeep of the ships. The treaty itself was only an uneasy truce: the legions were never given, and when in the autumn (37) Antony left Italy for Greece he had already reconsidered his position. So far, he had been loyal to all his agreements with Octavian; but he felt that Octavian had not been loyal to him. As he saw it, he had been shut out of Brundisium in 40, though Italy was common ground; Octavian had called him to a conference and had never appeared, and had asked for and then rejected his help; for two years he had been prevented from beginning the conquest of Parthia; his treaty right of recruiting in Italy was a dead letter; and now Octavian had his ships and he had not his legions. He had become convinced that further co-operation with Octavian was impossible; and a personal motive was reinforcing that conviction. He was tired of Octavia. He could not live on her level; his was a nature which no woman could hold unless she had something of the devil in her. His mind, reacting from Octavia's virtues, had gone back to a very different woman; memory, which glosses all defects, presented Cleopatra as more desirable even than the reality; he fell in love with her during, and perhaps because of, his absence from her. From Corcyra he sent Octavia back to Italy, for which her approaching confinement and his coming Parthian campaign provided an excuse, and summoned Cleopatra to meet him at Antioch. She came, and he married her forthwith; he had burnt his boats.

6. SICILY AND THE END OF SEXTUS POMPEIUS

Between the treaties of Brundisium and Tarentum a little less than three years had elapsed, yet actual peace in Italy lasted but an uneasy twelve months, and the troubler of it was, as before, Sextus Pompeius. Ancient historians were often unfair to unsuccessful candidates for power, and our sources combine to depict Sextus as the degenerate anti-thesis of his father, cruel and boorish, deficient alike in initiative and intellect, and wholly dependent on the brains of his Sicilian freedmen, Apollophanes, Demochares and Menas. In spite of the character of these sources—and much of Sextus' wickedness was perhaps that of the animal which, if attacked, defends itself—it is hard to find much in his favour. Neither before nor after Philippi had he the sense to co-operate with other anti-Caesarian leaders, and though the heritage of a great name attracted to him clients and nobles alike, he was unable to hold for long the loyalty of any Roman of note. His freedmen might win victories, but he himself had not enough energy or insight to follow them up. In all, his actions betray little beyond the limited purpose and outlook of a guerilla leader.[1] But at the time he had a genuine grievance: though Octavian acquiesced in yielding the islands to him, there was some difficulty over the transference of the Peloponnese, which was to come from Antony. Sextus declared that it had been granted him unconditionally and that Antony was deliberately lowering its value by extortion and taxation, to which Octavian replied that Antony had stipulated that Sextus should either pay over the tribute owing to him from Achaea or delay entry till it had been collected. Whatever the truth (and it looks as though there had been negligence on Antony's part), Sextus immediately let loose his pirate squadrons. Captured pirates confessed under torture that Sextus had instigated them, and Octavian determined on reprisals. To justify his action he published the terms of the treaty of Misenum; if war had to be made it would open

[1] Of Romans who joined with him, Sextus Bithynicus and Staius Murcus were treacherously murdered, Tiberius Nero left him in disgust, and most returned after the treaty of Misenum; after that, the only known Roman commanders are L. Plinius Rufus, Tisienus Gallus and, possibly, Cn. Cornelius Lentulus Cruscellio.

with advantage for him, since Menas (Sextus' governor in Sardinia) deserted, bringing over the island and three legions. In addition he was sure of the loyalty of two of the most important South Italian towns, Vibo and Rhegium, for he had exempted them from the assignations of 43 B.C. (p. 26), and had guaranteed their territories. To mark the end of the hollow pact with Sextus he divorced Scribonia ('utterly disgusted', as he wrote afterwards, 'with her contrary temper') on the very day that she bore him a daughter, Julia, who was destined to cause him more trouble than all her mother's tempers.

He now entered into an alliance very different from the coldly political one he had just thrown off, though this new one perhaps indicated a desire to appease and come nearer to that old senatorial aristocracy with whom Caesar had so signally failed. He had fallen in love passionately with Livia, the wife of Tiberius Nero, and the ardour of his passion no less than the complaisance with which Nero divorced his wife to give her to Octavian became a target for the wits of the day. The marriage took place on 17 January 38 B.C., three days after Livia had given birth to her second son Drusus; he and his three-year old brother Tiberius were to be reared in Octavian's house. Livia was nineteen, ambitious, beautiful, discreet; of aristocratic Republican stock, herself earlier a victim of the triumvirs' orders, she was a fit symbol of the reconciliation that was to come; throughout a devoted married life of fifty years she remained an influence for moderation and forgiveness.

Though Lepidus vouchsafed no reply to the appeals that Octavian sent out, Antony naturally promised help, and a meeting was arranged at Brundisium. Unfortunately, on the appointed day, Octavian did not turn up,[1] and Antony,

---

[1] This may possibly have been merely lateness on Octavian's part, due to some cause unknown; later he reproached Antony for not waiting longer.

declaring that Parthian affairs allowed no delay, returned
to Athens, leaving a curt message to Octavian not to violate
the pact. Sextus immediately interpreted this as proof that
Antony could not justify his colleague, and Octavian had
to assure the populace that he and Antony were in full
sympathy, and that Antony's reason for not surrendering
Achaea was his annoyance at Sextus' piracies. But the
events of the year went wholly in favour of the 'pirates'. The
plan of campaign was to invade Sicily in force: as Agrippa
was away in Gaul, Octavian appointed C. Calvisius Sabinus
as his admiral (with Menas under him), gathered legions
from Gaul and Illyricum, and ordered L. Cornificius to
bring a fleet from Ravenna to Tarentum. An action off
Cumae was indecisive, but Octavian, who had himself
brought Cornificius' fleet from Tarentum to Rhegium in
order to join with Calvisius, refused through excessive
caution to attack the smaller squadron of Sextus; as he was
sailing northwards through the Straits the ships of Sextus
flashed out and drove him back towards land, the rocky
promontories of Cape Scyllaeum; there followed a night
of confusion, and next morning a strong south wind turned
confusion into complete disaster. Octavian had lost half
his fleet and had to abandon any attempt on Sicily. Sextus'
exultation was correspondingly great; proclaiming himself
'son of Neptune' he offered sacrifices to his father, but
strangely enough made no effort to follow up his victory.

Though the year closed thus in humiliation for Octavian
the labours of his devoted friends gave promise of better
things for 37. The mob at Rome murmured against war, but
cities and well-wishers, to show their confidence, promised
money towards the construction of ships, and Maecenas,
who had journeyed to Greece in the previous autumn to
discuss disputed points with Antony, came back with the
glad assurance that he was willing to help. Best of all,

Agrippa returned from Gaul with a splendid record: he had been the second Roman general to lead troops across the Rhine, he had settled the Ubii on the site of Cologne and had won a brilliant victory over the insurgent Aquitani. He was to be consul for 37 and was offered a triumph, but with rare sympathy refused the coveted honour while his friend was in such distress. Octavian immediately entrusted him with the preparation and exercise of a fleet for next year, and ship-building was soon in full swing. As Italy did not possess a harbour or manœuvring area sufficiently spacious Agrippa crowned his work by making the famous roadstead of Lakes Lucrinus and Avernus and connecting the two lakes with the sea. Here there was ample room and for over a year freed slaves were practised at the oar, while experiments were carried out with a device of Agrippa's, whereby grap-nels were shot from a catapult to make it easier to hold and board an enemy ship. Even Lepidus finally consented to help.

As the spring of 37 B.C. was ending Antony duly appeared off Tarentum with 300 ships. He badly needed recruits for his Parthian campaigns, he could not obtain them without Octavian's co-operation, and he hoped to exchange ships for men. But Octavian hesitated: he was mistrustful and angry, he had heard that Antony was in negotiation with Lepidus, and confident in Agrippa and the new-built fleet he probably felt ashamed of his appeals for help in the previous year. Days passed. Octavia, in anguish, obtained leave from her husband to mediate between him and her brother; to each and every plaint or suspicion of Octavian's she had a sufficient reply, and thanks to her the two at last met near Tarentum. Twice she had saved Rome from civil war; a third time she was not to be so fortunate. But con-cord was restored: as the term fixed for the triumvirate by the Lex Titia had expired with the last day of 38 the two

agreed upon an extension of their powers;[1] they also agreed
to deprive Sextus Pompeius of what they had granted him,
and to give each other mutual assistance. Antony offered
120 ships from his fleet to Octavian and was in return
promised four legions; through Octavia's good offices her
brother received in addition ten *phaseli* and offered Antony
the choice of one thousand picked men from his bodyguard.
The two now parted: what happened to Antony and Octavia has already been told (pp. 65f.); in the West, though
preparations went on vigorously, Menas—vexed at being
kept in a subordinate position—returned to his old master,
Sextus, and Octavian used this as a pretext for depriving
Calvisius Sabinus of the command of the fleet and handing
it to Agrippa.

By the end of spring in 36 the time had come to put the
new fleet and new methods to a test, but operations did not
begin immediately. Octavian with characteristic caution
had prepared a complex scheme of attack, involving the
co-operation of three distinct fleets, and orders had to be
communicated and acknowledged; the campaign was to
begin on 1 July, the month of Julius Caesar. The plan was
that Agrippa with his fleet should smash the Sextian fleet
and render possible the invasion of Sicily in overwhelming
force; yet the crossing of the Straits against a resolute enemy
has always been a difficult problem and one to tax the genius

[1] The texts are notoriously contradictory. Dio says the triumvirate had
come to an end, Appian that it was coming to an end, and no reconciliation
was possible. The most reasonable hypothesis seems to the present writer to be
that the term fixed by the Lex Titia expired on 31 December 38 B.C., but that
all the triumvirs carried on, as they might do on the ground that their powers
could not lapse until they formally laid them down. At Tarentum Octavian
got Antony to agree to some form of extension, and later on tried to validate
that by getting a law passed granting a second five-year term. Henceforward, Octavian was careful to call himself triumvir *iterum* and emphasize
the constitutionality of his conduct, Antony simply continued to call himself
triumvir without any suggestion of a second term, and what Lepidus did is
unknown. See further, below, p. 117.

even of a Murat or a Garibaldi. Octavian was to start from Puteoli, Statilius Taurus with 102 ships from Tarentum (leaving some empty keels there), and Lepidus was to bring from Africa sixteen legions and 5000 horse. Against this formidable converging offensive Sextus had (at most) 300 warships and ten legions. He stationed himself at Messana with the best of his fleet and troops, and entrusted the defence of Lilybaeum and the west to L. Plinius Rufus. But he could not hold out long once Octavian's legions landed in the island; his main hope must lie in the capture or killing of the directing will behind the armament, Octavian himself.

The new fleet was solemnly purified, and on 1 July the three great expeditions started, to meet with very different fortunes. Lepidus landed twelve legions safely, blockaded Plinius in Lilybaeum, and overran the western half of Sicily.[1] On 3 July, however, a terrific storm burst over South Italy and Sicily and, though Taurus crept back discreetly to his base, Octavian met the full brunt of it. The damage would need a month at least to repair, the season was getting late, but Octavian did not relent. The crews of the shattered vessels were sent to fill the twenty-eight empty keels at Tarentum, Octavian went the round of the colonies and the veterans, and Maecenas hurried to Rome to allay the superstitions of the populace, who felt that Sextus had indeed the gods on his side. But Sextus again made no effort to exploit Neptune's favour, and Menas in disgust registered his third desertion.

Mid-August saw the attack resumed. This time Octavian made Vibo his headquarters; it was close to Sicily and within less than thirty miles (by land) of Scolacium, where Taurus now lay. Agrippa and his fleet were to attack Sicily from the north and keep Sextus' attention engaged, while

[1] Of four more legions following Lepidus two were cut off and destroyed by Demochares.

Octavian, helped by M. Valerius Messalla Corvinus (who had recently joined him) and by Statilius Taurus, was to transport his legions from Scolacium to Leucopetra, thence across to Tauromenium under cover of night, link up with Lepidus coming from the west, and fall on Messana; three legions under C. Carrinas at Columna Rhegia were to wait on events. But Sextus had learnt, or guessed, this plan of attack and made a skilful counter. Off Mylae Agrippa attacked a squadron under Demochares, and his larger and heavier-built ships had the advantage; Sextus sent reinforcements and finally appeared himself with the main body of his fleet; the Straits were left temptingly clear. Octavian seized the chance to ferry three legions across from Leucopetra and camped them on the lava spit of Naxos. The trap could now close: Sextus had managed to withdraw his ships in good order, Agrippa was resting his men. Before Octavian could return for the rest of the legions Sextus with fleet and cavalry swooped down upon him. Handing over the command of the three legions to L. Cornificius, Octavian decided to risk a sea-fight, but the superiority of Sextus' seamanship was crushingly demonstrated. Octavian's ships were burnt or wrecked, and though some survivors were rescued by Cornificius, Octavian himself only just managed to evade capture in the gathering darkness and reached the mainland with but one friend to be by him during the night. So near had Sextus come to success.

Octavian was utterly exhausted both in body and soul; for one moment even his will and belief broke and he begged his companion to kill him. His position was critical in the extreme: again Sextus had triumphed, Cornificius was isolated, he could not tell how Agrippa was faring, he could not be sure of Lepidus, for he was rumoured to have begun negotiations with Sextus; such was the outcome of five years' patient work. But dawn brought help and a renewal of hope; he was seen, recognized and escorted to Messalla. His first thought was for Cornificius and urgent messages were sent to Agrippa and all other commanders. Agrippa had by now attacked again, and had captured Tyndaris, one of the keys of the island; he threw out reconnoitring parties, and after a harassing march across the western slopes of Mt Aetna Cornificius and his three legions reached him unscathed.

The legions once securely in the island, the surrender of Sextus could be merely a matter of time; he was cooped up in the north-eastern corner, and while Lepidus and Octavian sat down to blockade Messana Taurus was dispatched to capture the towns that supplied him. Tradition records that the final battle took place after a challenge, as a result of which 300 ships from each side faced each other off Naulochus, while the troops watched from the shore. Though the incident of the challenge may be matched from the period it seems impossible that Sextus could muster 300 ships and the whole story smacks of rhetorical invention. However that may be, the final battle was fought on 3 September; the fight was long, but Agrippa's invention, the *harpax*, proved its value, and in the evening victory remained with the fleet of Octavian. Twenty-eight of Sextus' fleet were sunk, the rest were burnt or captured or ran aground, and only seventeen escaped to Messana. Sextus sent a desperate summons to Plinius Rufus to join him there, but time was short and without waiting for the arrival of his lieutenant he changed into civilian dress and with the remnant of his fleet fled from Sicily to throw himself on Antony's mercy; yet the ruling passion was strong even in flight and on the way he stopped to pillage the rich temple of Hera at Cape Lacinium. The rest of his career demands no long telling. Though he had sent envoys to Antony, the news of Roman failure in Media made him pause and he decided to offer

his services to the king of Parthia as well; these messengers
fell into Antony's hands, and though at first no active steps
were taken against him, he soon made himself so troublesome in Asia Minor that Titius, Antony's legate, had him
executed. It is possible that the fatal order was given by
Plancus, but it was Titius who had to bear the blame, and
the name of Pompey was still sufficiently revered in Rome
for the whole populace later to drive him from the theatre
by their execrations.

7. THE END OF THE CIVIL WARS

Victory, complete and definite, had come at last, thanks to
the skill and fidelity of Octavian's helpers, but due even
more to the indomitable tenacity he himself had exhibited.
Yet in the very hour of success a new menace faced him.
Lepidus, who had for years acquiesced perforce in his sub-
ordination, now judged himself strong enough to strike for
what he thought his rightful place. The large force with
which he had left Africa suggests that he had carefully
planned his *coup*, and now, while he and Agrippa combined
to urge the blockade of Messana, luck suddenly placed the
means and the moment in his hand. For Plinius, who had
taken charge of the city, offered to surrender: Agrippa ad-
vised waiting for the arrival of Octavian, who was at Naulochus, but Lepidus overrode him, accepted the surrender,
and then allowed his own fourteen legions to join with the
eight Sextian in plundering Messana during one long night
of licence. Next morning Octavian arrived to remonstrate,
but Lepidus, strong in the backing of twenty-two legions,
demanded the restoration of his rights and ordered Octavian to quit Sicily. The issue could not long be doubtful:
the soldiers were weary of civil war and still less inclined
to enter one for Lepidus, whose sluggishness they despised,

against Octavian, whose achievements were visible and splendid. Gradually they deserted, the Sextians first, then the men and officers of Lepidus' own legions, till at the last he was reduced to begging for mercy. Octavian spared his life but apparently forced him to resign his office of triumvir, and dismissed him to drag out the remainder of his days as Pontifex Maximus in honourable captivity at Circeii. His brief greatness was ended, and in the momentous developments of the next decade he was to take no share.

There now remained, crowded together into the northeastern corner of the island, a host of over forty legions; though their loyalties had been different, Sextian, Lepidan, or Caesarian, all were one in their longing for release from service and their numbers made them formidable indeed. Mutinous spirits fanned their discontent, and though Octavian reminded them of their oath and offered promises, they clamoured for something more substantial, for instant and profitable dismissal. But one of their ringleaders, a centurion, mysteriously disappeared, his fate deterred others, and finally Octavian disbanded twenty thousand, who had fought at Mutina and Philippi, and bestowed bounties on the rest with promise of early demobilization. Tribunes and centurions were given the rank of decurion in their native town, and Agrippa, for his magnificent services, was awarded a *corona rostrata*—a golden crown adorned with ships' prows—an honour never bestowed before. Finally Octavian arranged for the settlement of the territories that had fallen to him: of Sardinia little is known, though a colony was apparently founded at Turris Libisonis; in Sicily a colony was planted at Tauromenium, and though Catana, Centuripa and Syracuse were rewarded for good service during the war, the other Sicilian cities had to face a demand for sixteen hundred talents. The former Sextian commanders were pardoned, and runaway slaves restored

to their masters. After a year spent in pacifying Sicily Statilius Taurus crossed over to organize the two provinces of
Africa.

Having made the necessary arrangements Octavian could
at last return to Rome, and his return was a triumphal progress, for nobles and commons alike flocked out in festal
garlands and dress to escort him into the city. He did not
however enter until 13 November, when he celebrated the
ovatio which the Senate had decreed, but in the meantime
other honours had been crowded upon him by a grateful
people. The anniversary of Naulochus was to be a festival,
a triumphal arch was to be erected, and a golden statue set
up with an inscription celebrating the restoration of peace
after long disturbances on sea and land. An official residence was voted to him, close to the ground which he himself reserved for a temple to his patron deity Apollo. Like
his father he was given the right of wearing the laurel-
wreath of the conqueror, and, most important of all, he was
granted a sacrosanctity similar to that enjoyed by the tribunes—a privilege which two years later he had conferred
upon his wife and sister (see also p. 150). Thus already his
own person was marked out as something hallowed and
eminent, and this tribunician sacrosanctity foreshadowed
the *potestas tribunicia* which was to be one of the great props
of the coming principate.

The long horror of the civil wars was over, peace and
prosperity should return once more—such was the burden
of the speeches which Octavian made to the Senate and
the People, in which he defended his acts as due to the
necessity of the times. In conformity with these utterances
he remitted a large number of public debts, cancelled some
taxes, burnt the documents relating to the civil wars, and
hinted that the Republican constitution would be restored
when Antony returned from his Parthian campaigns. Too

long had Roman fought against Roman; the time had come
to turn against the barbarian. These speeches were not
meant only for Rome; they had a message for all Italy,
for Octavian published and circulated them throughout
the peninsula: men could labour on their farms and homes
in security, all could return to the normal business of life.
The famine and misery produced by Sextus' raids and inter-
ception of the corn-supply had taught one lesson, the depen-
dence of Italy upon foreign corn. It cannot be coincidence
only that Varro's treatise upon agriculture appeared in
36 B.C. and that while an imperial freedman, Hyginus, was
compiling practical handbooks for farmers in plain prose,
Virgil at the prompting of Maccenas was beginning with
loving care the great epic of the Italian countryside, the
Georgics.

Caesar's murder had been avenged, his last enemies
routed, but for the man who had accepted Caesar's heritage a loftier task remained. Whatever projects Caesar may
have had for the East, his main achievement—whether as
general or statesman—had been in the West, in Spain and
Gaul and Italy. Octavian's reverence for Italian tradition
and religion was deep implanted—as witness his refusal to
take the office of Pontifex Maximus from Lepidus—and
during nine long years of schooling he had grown to see
what Italy and the Empire needed and to believe that he
was fated to give it. Time and again he had been near death,
from illness or enemies, yet his life had always been spared,
and the consciousness that destiny was guarding him for a
great work must have been continually strengthened.[1] This
consciousness and this singleness of purpose explain the devotion that he was able to inspire in his peers; the ordinary

[1] From the fragments of his autobiography it looks as though Octavian
himself laid special stress upon these escapes and the notion of a special
providence preserving him.

soldier might be fascinated by the magic of a splendid name, but it was something high and essential in the man himself that bound men of the calibre of Agrippa and Maecenas in such unquestioning and selfless loyalty or gained the respect and service of the Republican Messalla Corvinus, or of Statilius Taurus and others who were won over to his side. Because he stood for something more than mere ambition he could draw a nation to him in the coming struggle.

For struggle there must be. The Roman realm now lay in the hands of two men; the statutory triumvirate had dwindled to an unauthorized duovirate. Octavian's treatment of Lepidus—little though his lethargic personality had counted in the coalition—and appropriation of the provinces of Sicily and Africa could not be defended on any constitutional grounds and could not be overlooked by Antony, even though his own conduct had not been impeccable. Herein lay dangerous chances of dissension between characters so disparate, and the influence Octavia might exert for peace was more than balanced by the imperial designs of Cleopatra. In that struggle few could foretell the result. The legions, weary of interminable fighting, would not always follow a leader's ambition against countrymen and comrades: the victor must possess not merely name or prestige, but above all a cause and a battle-cry that would rally waverers to his side and convince not only soldiers but citizens also that the unity of the Roman world was at stake.

III

THE WAR OF THE EAST
AGAINST THE WEST

I. CLEOPATRA AND ANTONY

Antony's marriage to Cleopatra in the autumn of 37 was the turning-point of his career, the beginning of his breach with the West. He did not propose to attack Octavian; he merely meant to go his own way without reference to his colleague. His preoccupation at present was Parthia: its conquest would prove him Caesar's true heir and would outweigh any prestige Octavian could acquire. But his marriage had no connection with this scheme of conquest. Egypt was wealthy; but he drew nothing from Egypt for his invasion of Parthia, of which Cleopatra disapproved (p. 95); and the modern belief that he married her for her money is certainly untrue. Had it been money, he had only to raise his hand and she was dethroned and Egypt and the money his, amid Roman applause; he could not do it, because he had fallen in love with her. For this he married her, though he knew that it meant a general assent to her point of view. For the shock to Roman opinion he now cared nothing; and however strongly one condemns his treatment of Octavia, one must also sympathize with his scorn of an outlook which had no objection to the queen as his mistress but every objection to her as his wife. He married her in the form the Ptolemies used, presumably the Macedonian, and to every one east of the Adriatic she was his legitimate wife; but, as a Roman citizen, he could not in Roman law either have two wives at once or contract a valid marriage with a

foreigner,[1] and this enabled Octavian for the present, whatever he felt, to take no official notice of the marriage.
Antony's is a strange story. Two women had been devoted
to him. Had he followed Fulvia, he might perhaps have
been master of the Roman world; had he followed Octavia,
he could have ruled his half in peace, too popular to be
attacked. Instead, he had broken Fulvia's heart and made
Octavia homeless. Now he had married a woman whose
only devotion to him was as the instrument of her ambition;
and her he would follow, and follow to his ruin, because he
loved her. That is what redeems his memory, that at the
end he did lose half the world for love.

Cleopatra had acted as though she expected his summons,
and she started to build up a position which should end in
her being what she had hoped to have been had Caesar
lived. She took the upper hand at once, as at Tarsus, and
requested a royal wedding-gift, the foreign empire of her
great predecessor Ptolemy II. Antony gave her all he could.
He executed Lysanias for his treason in 40 and gave her
Lysanias' kingdom of Chalcis, together with everything between Chalcis and Herod's realm (Hippos and Gadara are
expressly mentioned); it was the old Coele-Syria in the
narrower sense, and comprised all central Syria. He gave
her the greater part of the coast of Palestine and Phoenicia
from Egypt to the river Eleutherus, the original Ptolemaic
boundary; Tyre and Sidon alone remained free cities. He
gave her Cyprus, which had once been Roman territory,
but had already been alienated by Caesar. And he took
from Polemo Cilicia Tracheia, which had likewise once
been Roman territory, and gave it to her also (except the
city of Seleuceia), so that she might get ship-timber from

---

[1] The controversy whether Antony had two wives at once or not is
misconceived. In every law but Roman he had, in Roman law he
had not.

the Taurus, as Arsinoe II had done. The former Ptolemaic possessions on the Aegean being out of the question, there now remained only Judaea and Galilee, which were Herod's, and the one-time Ptolemaic part of Nabataea. She begged hard for Herod's kingdom, but here Antony was adamant, and all she got was Herod's deadly enmity. But he gave her the best morsel of Herod's realm, the balsam gardens of Jericho with the balsam monopoly, and (it seems) what of Nabataea Ptolemy II had had—the land east of the Dead Sea with the monopoly of the bitumen fishery, so important to Egypt. Nabataea, Egypt's secular enemy, was not really a client-state; but Malchus would hardly venture to oppose Antony. The son whom Cleopatra bore in the autumn of 36, when Antony was in Media, was named by her Ptolemy Philadelphus, to commemorate her re-establishment of Philadelphus' empire.

Antony was popular in Alexandria, where it was remembered that he had once prevented Ptolemy Auletes from killing his Alexandrian prisoners; and Cleopatra presently began to build a temple to him, which was unfinished at her death and was turned into one to Augustus. She and Antony put each other's heads on their coins (she was the only Ptolemaic queen who coined in her own right); and since Antony had already, for a very different reason, proclaimed himself Dionysus (pp. 66, 87), they were able to pose as a divine pair, as the Hellenistic East expected. To Greeks they were Dionysus and Aphrodite, to Egyptians Osiris and Isis. To Antony this was a deliberate political measure, but to Cleopatra it was probably something more. Her attitude towards the religion of Egypt has already been indicated, and just as her death shows that she believed herself to be a daughter of Re, so she perhaps took herself seriously as Isis; she wore her robes on state occasions, and in disputes in other kingdoms she sided with the woman—

with Aba at Olba, Alexandra in Judaea—as became one who was Isis, goddess and champion of women.

Cleopatra had brought her twins to Antioch, and when Antony married her he acknowledged them as his and renamed them Alexander Helios and Cleopatra Selene, the Sun and the Moon. The names of all Cleopatra's children are significant, but especially that of Alexander Helios. Helios and Selene in conjunction possibly had a political meaning; the Parthian king was 'Brother of the Sun and Moon', and if the sun and moon really typified the Iranian *fravashi* and *hvareno*, Antony, by annexing these luminaries to his own family, was perhaps symbolically depriving Phraates of the supernatural adjuncts of his royalty. As to the name Helios, Antony's coin-type after Philippi had been the Sun radiate, and his momentary revival of that type late in 37 shows that he was passing on to the boy whatever the Sun meant to himself. Probably it meant to him the supreme deity of Asia, but it had other connotations also; an Egyptian oracle had derived prosperity from the Sun, in the prophecy of the Cumaean Sibyl the rule of the Sun was to precede the Golden Age, and for Greeks Iambulus, in the story of his Sun-state, had definitely connected the age of gold with the Sun. As, in addition, it was Cleopatra's privilege, as a New Isis, to bear the Sun, and as she herself was the Sun-god's daughter, the boy could not really be called anything else; he was the Sun-child who should inaugurate the Golden Age. The name Alexander referred primarily to Antony's coming conquest of Parthia. Antony, like many Romans, had dreamt of being a new Alexander—had he not at Philippi covered Brutus' body with his purple cloak?[1]—but this too he now transferred to the boy, and became himself only the warrior king who should precede the king of the Golden Age and

[1] As Alexander had covered the body of Darius.

pacify the earth with his sword. But there was more than this. In the writer's view, Virgil's Fourth Eclogue was an epithalamium for the marriage of Antony and Octavia, and the child who should be a new Alexander and inaugurate the Golden Age was the son to be born to them. A coin of Antony's may reflect this union of the two houses; but the child of the Eclogue had never been born, for Octavia's child had been a girl, and that is why after its birth Antony returned to the idea of Asiatic conquest, proclaimed himself Dionysus, conqueror of Asia, and did his best for Octavia by putting her head on his Dionysus coinage. But when he left Octavia for Cleopatra, the whole symbolism was transferred. Though his assumption of divinity as Dionysus had been connected with Octavia, not with Cleopatra, it now fell most conveniently, for Dionysus could be Osiris and he and Cleopatra could be the divine pair Osiris-Isis; and Virgil's ideas could, through the boy's name, be transferred to Cleopatra's son, for whom they were never meant, but whom they fitted well, for he was the destined king of a golden age (though not of Virgil's) and a new Alexander, and he was *cara deum suboles*, the dear offspring of the gods Antony-Dionysus and Cleopatra-Isis, who would rule an Asia pacified by his father's valour. These are some of the ideas which seem to play round the name of the boy who was never to fulfil his destiny; how one Greek in the East was to envisage the coming age of gold will appear later (p. 104).

Antony spent the winter of 37–6 at Antioch with Cleopatra, not in amusement, but in strenuous preparation for the Parthian campaign. Before starting he had to secure his rear. Syria south of the Roman province was safe in the hands of Cleopatra and of Herod; but Antony now undertook the long-delayed reorganization of Asia Minor (was the impulse Cleopatra's?), and used to the full his new liberty of choosing the best men without regard to dynastic considerations. His system in Asia Minor was built up on three men, Amyntas, Archelaus, and Polemo. The strong Amyntas, who was already ruling western Pisidia and Phrygia-toward-Pisidia, was made king of Galatia and also received Lycaonia and part of Pamphylia; this, with his existing Pisidian kingdom, placed the whole centre of Asia Minor in one hand. The Galatian cavalry, the best in the Roman East, was valuable to Antony, and at some period he rewarded two Galatian chieftains: Adiatorix with the rule of the Roman part of Heraclea and Ateporix with part of Zelitis. He executed Ariarathes of Cappadocia for his treason in 40 and gave Cappadocia to Archelaus of Comana, but without Armenia Minor. Archelaus was a student and writer of the type of Juba II; and while previous kings of Cappadocia had called themselves 'Friends of Rome', he called himself Philopatris, 'Friend of his country'. Polemo's kingdom of Cilicia Tracheia had been given by Antony to Cleopatra, but Eastern Pontus was apparently vacant, which may mean that Darius was dead. Antony now sent Polemo to Pontus, but gave him much more than Darius' realm; he reconstituted for him the old kingdom of Pontus from Armenia to the Halys, which gave him part of the Roman province of 'Bithynia and Pontus', and he added to it Armenia Minor,[1] which carried the wardenship of the Upper Euphrates. Of Antony's four important discoveries who now ruled the principal client-kingdoms—Herod of Judaea, Amyntas of Galatia, Archelaus of Cappadocia, and Polemo of Pontus—all had successful reigns from the Roman point of view, and all but Amyntas (who was

---

[1] Dio says that Polemo did not get Armenia Minor till 34. As this frontier province could not have been left vacant for three years, this would mean that Antony gave it to Archelaus in 37 and took it from him in 34, which seems impossible.

killed in war in 25 B.C.) had very long ones. At Olba in Cilicia Cleopatra restored Aba, a Teucrid by marriage, to the priest-kingship; it had been usurped by her father Zeno-phanes, a local tyrant who was not of the royal line.

In spring 36 Antony left Syria to join his army; Cleopatra, who was expecting the birth of Ptolemy Philadelphus, accompanied him to Zeugma and then returned to Egypt. On her way back she visited Herod, to arrange about her monopolies; doubtless she enjoyed the knowledge that her courteous host, a barbarian beneath his varnish, would have killed her but for the certainty of Antony's vengeance. She understood business; she leased to Herod his balsam gardens for 200 talents a year, and she leased the bitumen monopoly to Malchus for a similar rent and made Herod guarantee it and collect it for her; the arrangement would cause bad blood between her two enemies. Herod paid punctually, for he dared not do otherwise, but after Antony's failure in Media he got little from Malchus. He seemingly took a belated revenge upon Cleopatra by stating in his *Memoirs* that she made love to him, so that, should he trip, she might force Antony to kill him; naturally Herod upon Cleopatra is not evidence, and the story is certainly untrue.

Herod had begun his reign by making one Ananel High Priest; but Alexandra had asked Cleopatra to use her in-fluence with Antony for her son, the young Aristobulus, grandson of Aristobulus II and last male representative of the Hasmonaean line. Early in 36 Herod did make Aristo-bulus High Priest, whether because Antony requested it or because he wished to conciliate the Hasmonaean interest. Whether Alexandra subsequently began to intrigue for the crown for her son is uncertain; but that autumn she thought that she and the boy were in danger, and sought Cleopatra's help. Cleopatra sent a ship to bring them to Egypt, but their attempt at flight was frustrated. The people, however,

showed such favour to the boy that late that year, Antony
being far away, Herod had him murdered. Alexandra he
did not touch, it is said through fear of Cleopatra, and she
again appealed to the queen, this time for vengeance. When
in January 35 Cleopatra met Antony in Syria on his return
from the Parthian expedition (p. 95) she urged him to
punish Herod, but though Antony sent for Herod, he had
too much trouble on his hands to think of removing his loyal
and capable supporter, and yielded to his argument that,
as he had been made king, he must be allowed to act as such.

2. THE INVASION OF PARTHIA

In 38–7 a new king ascended the Parthian throne. Orodes, broken by the death of his beloved son Pacorus, had
made another son, Phraates (IV), his heir; but the old man
died slowly, and Phraates murdered him and seized the
crown. He is called cruel, and he had trouble with his
nobles; some he killed, others fled from Parthia. But the
trouble was probably connected with the same difficulty
which had brought down Surenas, the jealousy between
noble and commoner, cataphract and horse-archer. The
nobles had had their chance against Ventidius and had
failed completely, and Phraates meant to rely on the horse-
archers against Antony; fortunately for Parthia he was
strong enough to have his way. He had the support, among
others, of Monaeses, the powerful Warden of the Western
Marches, who owned great estates in Mesopotamia and was
designated for the supreme command. Monaeses played
the common trick of fleeing to Antony in simulated fear
and offering him his services, with a view to discovering
his plans. Antony welcomed him, gave him the one-time
kingdom of Alchaudonius, and promised him the throne
of Parthia, but whether he was really deceived does not

appear; certainly Monaeses did not inform him of Parthia's change of tactics. In spring 36 Monaeses suddenly lost his fear of Phraates and returned to Parthia to take command; throughout the war Phraates never took the field himself.

Antony was a good tactician and cavalry leader, but he had never tried to plan a great campaign. As he had Caesar's papers, none could gainsay his claim to be carrying out Caesar's scheme; but it is certain that he was not. Caesar no doubt had meant to strike at the Parthian capital Ecbatana through Armenia, but he would never have left an uncertain ally of some power between himself and his base; even Crassus had been too wise to do that. Caesar presumably meant first to reduce Armenia and create there an advanced base; after that, it may be conjectured that he intended to take Ecbatana and cut off Babylonia from Parthia proper, and finally to annex Babylonia and establish his new frontier. But Antony, who had been prevented for two years by events in Italy from making a start, had become impatient and perhaps tried to do too much the first year, though it is not known whether it was early or late in 37 that Canidius Crassus was sent to carry out the preliminary conquest of Armenia; if the latter, Antony had in mind Alexander's winter campaigns. Canidius defeated Artavasdes in a battle, and the king, who had been Parthia's ally since 53, formally submitted and again became the ally of Rome. Either Canidius or Antony was mad enough to think that this sufficed; there were no guarantees—no towns were occupied, no hostages taken, no garrisons left. In spring 36 Canidius passed on and, like Pompey, reduced the Albani and Iberi of the Caucasus, and Antony struck a coin with the Armenian tiara as though Armenia were his. Armenia's regular policy was to maintain independence by playing off Parthia against Rome, but as between them her sympathies, like her civilization, were Parthian. Artavasdes had lightly

deserted Rome in 53, and though he submitted to Antony
he maintained an understanding with Phraates. Antony
had failed before he started, for his preparations had
thoroughly alarmed Asia. The other Artavasdes, king of
Media Atropatene (hereinafter called Media), had joined
Parthia, as perhaps Elymaïs did also; Asia was closing her
ranks against the Roman, and Armenia could not well hold
aloof.

Early in May 36 Antony left Zeugma and went northwards through Melitene and along the Euphrates to Carana
(Erzerûm), where Canidius joined him. Our sources imply
that he started too late, but it was no use reaching Carana
before Canidius was ready. At Carana he reviewed his
army, the best he ever commanded. He had left seven
legions in Macedonia and one at Jerusalem, but none in
Syria. In face of his attack, Parthia could hardly spare men
for a diversion on the Euphrates. He had sixteen seasoned
legions of about three-quarter strength, totalling 60,000
men; 10,000 Gallic and Spanish horse; and 30,000 auxili-
aries, which included Artavasdes with some 16,000 Armenian cavalry and the forces of some client-kings; among his
legates were Domitius and Canidius, and Plancus' nephew
Titius was quaestor. He brought an enormous siege-train,
including an 80-foot ram, for he was going to operate in a
country devoid of good timber. The large force of legions
shows both that he expected to meet the cataphracts and
that he meant to garrison Ecbatana and other towns till
Phraates submitted; there was no question of one summer sufficing. His first objective was the Median capital
Phraaspa, on his road to Ecbatana; but whether he hoped
to reach Ecbatana before winter, or meant to winter in
Media, cannot be said.

Leaving Carana, he marched through the open country
east of Lake Urumia, but his train of wagons, extending for

many miles, made progress slow, and he divided his army. He left Artavasdes, Polemo, and Oppius Statianus with two legions to escort the wagons, and pushed on ahead with his main force. Alexander too had sometimes divided his army; but he had always left his best general and a majority of the troops with the wagons. Moreover, Antony was marching blind; he had no idea where the Parthian army might be, while Monaeses had accurate information of his movements, proof of Artavasdes' understanding with Phraates. Monaeses, in fact, with 40,000 horse-archers, and the Median king, with another 10,000, were quite close: the subsequent campaign shows that they must have had some system of a reserve of arrows. With their perfect intelligence they eluded Antony and came down on the wagons. Artavasdes, whose troops formed the greater part of the escort, rode off home before the attack; the two legions were annihilated and their eagles added to the Parthian collection; Polemo was captured by the Medes; the siege-train was burnt, the food burnt or carried off. The victory was as decisive as could be, and Antony found himself in mid-August helpless before Phraaspa, a strong fortress well garrisoned and provisioned.

But he was too proud to retreat. He threw up a mound against the wall, but his attacks were repulsed, and what machines he could improvise proved useless. The army soon ate up all the food in the neighbourhood and had to go far afield, while the Parthians shot down every weak foraging party. As a last resource Antony offered battle; Monaeses accepted, but could not shake the legions and just rode away again. Antony claimed a victory, but the Parthians only lost 80 killed, and meanwhile the garrison in a sortie had burnt his machines. It was now October, and the cold was beginning; even his stubbornness had to recognize that retreat was inevitable. The story that, at some time after the equinox, he sent envoys to Phraates, who received them seated on the golden throne of the Arsacids (which was in Ecbatana) and promised them peace if they retired, seems impossible, in view of the time needed to reach Ecbatana and return; for the retreat cannot have begun later than mid-October. A Mardian deserter, one of his race settled in Media, offered to guide the Romans back by a different way, avoiding the plains; Antony wisely accepted and the man saved them, taking them through the hills by Tabriz.

The terrible retreat to the Armenian frontier lasted 27 days. The army marched in square; in spite of the hilly ground, Monaeses hung on its rear, cut off stragglers and foragers, and attacked at every opportunity. There were frequent desertions, and though the slingers made themselves respected in skirmishes there was one regular battle in which the Romans had 8000 casualties. They suffered from disease, thirst, and hunger, and ate 'unspeakable food'; but through it all the veterans remained too steady to be overwhelmed. The danger brought out all that was best in Antony; once more, and for the last time, he was the Antony of the retreat from Mutina, the worshipped leader who shared every privation and never lost heart. One night the army did get out of hand and he prepared for suicide, but in the morning he recovered control. At last, at a river six days from the frontier, the victorious Parthians turned back, after shouting a tribute to their enemies' courage; they had established a tradition of the invincibility of Parthia in defence which lasted till Trajan. It may or may not have been a consequence of his victory that Phraates appears later in Greek poems from Susa as 'god omnipotent', a unique title quite outside the sphere of the Mazdean religion.

On entering Armenia Antony sent off a message to Cleopatra, which somehow reached her. He could not winter in that hostile country; he would have had to divide his army into detachments and would have courted the fate of Antiochus Sidetes. He spoke Artavasdes fair, for there was no alternative, and got food; and the worn-out men started afresh on their long march through the snow-bound land. He stayed with them till he was sure that Artavasdes would not attack them, and then, like Napoleon from Russia, pushed on ahead, leaving Canidius and Domitius to bring the army home. Syria might already be in Parthian hands and every city in revolt; that was why he had told Cleopatra to meet him, not at one of the great seaports, but at Leuke Kome, a village where she could force a landing. Even though he found Syria safe he was terribly anxious, for he did not know in what temper the army might arrive; it was only an army of the Civil Wars, whose allegiance sat lightly on it; it had already mutinied once, and in fact another 8000 men died in the Armenian snows. The story goes that day after day at Leuke Kome he would rush from dinner to scan the horizon for the Egyptian ships. But Cleopatra did not fail him; dangerous as winter navigation was, she arrived in time, bringing what he had asked for—masses of clothing and comforts for the troops; thanks to this help, the army was got quietly into winter quarters. But she brought little money; though Antony somehow supplemented it, it only sufficed to give the men some 28 shillings apiece. It was her method of explaining to him that her treasury was not at his service for useless adventures. His expedition had indeed been worse than useless; he had lost some 37 per cent of his army, including over 22,000 of his veteran legionaries. True, Xenophon had lost nearly as high a percentage on his much-praised retreat from Cunaxa to Trapezus, and he had not had to face Parthian arrows. But to Antony the loss was irreparable; he could get no more seasoned Roman troops, and probably the men who did return were never quite the same again. Meanwhile Octavian had conquered Sextus and removed Lepidus, and controlled forty-five legions.

3. THE DREAM OF EMPIRE

Antony returned to Alexandria with Cleopatra and sat down to consider the position. Octavian might send the promised four legions, which would largely replace his losses; but any illusions on that subject were dispelled in the early spring, when Octavian sent him, not the legions, but what remained (70) of his 130 ships. Octavian's policy must have seemed to them clear: cut off from recruiting in Italy, Antony's power was to die like a ring-barked tree; Octavian only had to wait till the tree fell of itself. Cleopatra seized her opportunity. The sequel shows that it was now that she won Antony over to her own scheme. Parthia (she must have argued) mattered nothing; his enemy was Octavian. Sooner or later he would have to fight him, and he must mobilize all his resources for one great effort while success was still possible; that victory once won, Parthia or anything else he wanted would follow. Doubtless she knew that it was very late in the day and that the chances were against them; but it was the only chance she had had since Caesar's death of realizing her supreme ambition of ruling the Roman world,[1] and, whatever the odds, her courage was equal to taking that chance. She had of course no more right to conquer Rome, supposing she could, than Octavian had to conquer Egypt, but she had a right to resent Rome's treatment of her country and her line. It had broken the spirit of her predecessors, but it did not break hers. But she

[1] Her son's name, Ptolemy-who-is-also-Caesar, and her oath witness to this ambition. It was believed by Romans, by Jews, and, more important, by a Greek who supported her (see p. 104). But the best evidence is the actions of herself and Antony, pp. 101 ff.

could only work through Antony; that was why she had married him. Her design of attacking Rome by means of Romans was one of such stupendous audacity that we must suppose that she saw no other way. There was indeed an alternative—to try and raise a semi-religious Graeco-Asiatic crusade; this was what Rome feared,[1] but we cannot say whether she considered it, though Virgil, who made the whole of the Asia of the Alexander tradition—Bactria, India, Sabaea—follow her to Actium, shows that some Romans thought she did. As for Antony, had he himself ever desired to oust Octavian he would never have let Sextus and Lepidus fall as he had done, and his inactivity during 33, a wasted year, shows that his heart was not in the business. He was being driven on by two stronger natures, on the one side Cleopatra, on the other Octavian, and all Cleopatra's gifts of both mind and person must have been lavished on securing his assent. He had, however, first to punish Artavasdes for his treason; both knew that to be imperative.

Antony had written to Italy that the Parthians had been defeated, and Rome held festival accordingly; but Octavian knew the truth, as did his sister. Octavia held that Antony's purported marriage with a foreign woman did not make herself any the less his wife; it was enough that he needed help, and in March 35, as soon as navigation opened, she started to go to him, as Cleopatra had done, with large stores of clothing and necessaries for his army and 2000 picked men given her by her brother. Probably the troops really were meant as an invitation to Antony to leave Cleopatra and return to Octavia; Aeneas' treatment of Dido, who in some aspects recalls Cleopatra, may show

[1] There is not the least indication anywhere that Rome ever feared Antony; Rome can hardly, therefore, have feared Cleopatra's influence over him.

what kind of conduct was expected of him. Octavia reached
Athens, and there found a message from Antony ordering
her to send on her troops and supplies and go back herself
to Rome. It was brutal; a man between two women is
likely to be brutal. She obeyed, and went back. Octavian,
naturally furious, told her to leave Antony's house, but she
refused; as his wife, her place was there till he himself told
her to go. So she stayed, and looked after his political
interests and his children; not only her own two daughters,
but also Fulvia's two sons, whom she had taken charge of,
though the elder soon afterwards went to Antony. The sight
of her unselfish goodness did Antony much harm in Italy,
though to harm him was the last thing she would have
wished.

Probably Antony meant to rest his troops for some months
and invade Armenia in summer 35; but he lost that year
through Sextus Pompeius, whose activities in Asia compelled Antony to send against him the legions from Syria
under Titius (p. 77). Titius ultimately hunted him down
and killed him, whether with or without Antony's knowledge. It shows Antony's changed position that the surviving murderers of Caesar, Turullius and Cassius of Parma,
who had been with Sextus, now joined him. Antony could
not ask his troops to do any more that season; but he began
to arm. He had now twenty-five legions, some very weak
in numbers: seven in Macedonia, thirteen in Syria (including one at Jerusalem), two in Syria or Bithynia, and
three mixed legions of recruits taken from Sextus. He raised
five more, giving him thirty in all. He could get some
Italians from Caesar's colonies and the numerous Italian
traders, but the inscriptions show that he also enlisted many
Asiatics or Greeks, who took Latin names. Following
Caesar's practice, he did not fill up the gaps in the legions
of the Parthian campaign, using his recruits solely for the

new legions; but he brought from Macedonia six of the veteran legions there, now the strongest he had, and replaced them by six legions of recruits. He also started shipbuilding on a great scale, and began to strike thirty series of coins, each giving the number of one of his thirty legions and on the reverse his flagship. He further flouted Roman opinion by marrying his daughter Antonia (by his first wife) to a wealthy Greek, Pythodorus of Tralles; their daughter was the notable Pythodoris.

The Parthians had not invaded Syria after Antony's retreat because, with the external danger removed, internal troubles had broken out again; Phraates' dated tetradrachms fail from 36 to April 34. Also they had quarrelled with the Medes over the booty, and the Median king, in anger and fear, released Polemo and sent him to Antony with an offer of his alliance against Parthia. Antony had no intention of attacking Parthia again, but he welcomed the alliance as proof that his expedition had not been fruitless. This was the position when early in 34 Antony, who on 1 January had taken and laid down the consulship, invaded Armenia, mastered the country, and captured Artavasdes and his younger sons Tigranes and Artavasdes; the eldest son, Artaxes, escaped and tried to raise the people, but was defeated and fled to Phraates. Antony gave a section of Armenia to the Median king and betrothed Alexander Helios to that monarch's little daughter Iotape. A story remains that he only captured Artavasdes by inviting him to a friendly conference and then seizing him— 'Antony's crime'; but as Octavian is also accused of having instigated Artavasdes' treachery towards Antony, the two stories are obviously charge and counter-charge in the propaganda war of 33 and are both untrue. For two years Armenia became a Roman province, and 'Roman' traders, i.e. subjects of Rome, flocked into it. Antony left his legions to winter there and returned to Alexandria before autumn, bringing with him Artavasdes and his sons and much booty, including the solid gold statue of Anaitis from her temple in Acilisene. The effect of his arming was now seen, for the reason was known or guessed at Rome, and while Rome had celebrated his earlier successes she ignored the conquest of Armenia; it was as though he were no longer her general.

The subsequent developments beyond the Euphrates may be anticipated here. Early in 33, in response to an urgent message, Antony again hurried to the Median frontier and saw the king, who feared a Parthian attack. He restored his share of the Roman eagles, and possibly Antony, who took Iotape back with him as hostage, gave him temporary help, for he did not withdraw his legions from Armenia till the autumn; but the Mede really secured himself for a time by an alliance with Tiridates. Tiridates, perhaps a general of Phraates in the war with Antony,[1] revolted in 32 or early 31, and in summer 31 expelled Phraates; but Phraates came back in 30 with help from 'Scythians', probably the Sacaraucae, and Tiridates, who was not an Arsacid, could not maintain himself. He and the Median king fled to Syria (p. 144), then in Octavian's hands, and Phraates took Media and also restored Artaxes to the Armenian throne.[2] Artaxes promptly massacred all the Roman traders in Armenia, and that country and Media were definitely lost to Rome.

To come back to the main story, in the autumn of 34, after Antony's return from the conquest of Armenia, Alexandria witnessed two extraordinary spectacles. Antony staged a triumph in the city, a thing hardly ever before celebrated

[1] Conceivably he was Monaeses, but the matter is too uncertain to build on.

[2] An undated tetradrachm of Phraates IV, overstruck on a coin of Attambelos I, shows that at some time Phraates reconquered Characene, which may therefore have been Tiridates' ally; but this more probably belongs to Tiridates' second attempt in 27–26.

by a Roman except in Rome. High above the people Cleopatra sat in state on a golden throne, and Antony entered
the city in a triumphal car, followed in procession by his
Armenian captives, whom he presented to the queen. The
presiding deity of a Roman triumph was Jupiter Optimus
Maximus of the Capitol as the embodiment of Rome; and,
whatever Antony may have meant,[1] men naturally saw in
his act the glorification of Cleopatra as an embodiment of
the 'goddess Rome', and attributed to him (almost certainly
wrongly) the intention of shifting the capital from Rome to
Alexandria. In one other respect his triumph differed from
the Roman form: he spared Artavasdes' life, even though
he had been a traitor.

The triumph was followed by the ceremony generally
known as the Donations of Alexandria. A great concourse
of people gathered in the gymnasium;[2] above them Antony,
and Cleopatra robed as Isis, sat on thrones side by side, and
somewhat lower, on other thrones, sat their three children
and Ptolemy Caesar (whom Alexandrians nicknamed Caesarion, little Caesar). Antony first harangued the people;
he said that Cleopatra had been Caesar's wife (i.e. by a
Macedonian marriage), that Ptolemy Caesar was Caesar's
legitimate son, and that what he was going to do was a
tribute to Caesar's memory. He then declared Cleopatra
Queen of Kings and Ptolemy Caesar King of Kings, joint
monarchs of Egypt and Cyprus and overlords of the kingdoms or overlordships of Cleopatra's other children. To
Alexander, who wore the dress of the Achaemenid kings
and received an Armenian bodyguard, he gave as his kingdom Armenia and the overlordship of Parthia and Media,

---

[1] Possibly he had in mind the triumphal procession of Ptolemy II. In
any case, Hellenistic influences were affecting the Roman triumph.

[2] Had Alexandria had a Senate it must (it would seem) have been mentioned as playing some part in this ceremony.

that is, everything east of the Euphrates. To Ptolemy Philadelphus, who wore Macedonian dress and received a Macedonian bodyguard, he gave as his kingdom the Egyptian
possessions in Syria and Cilicia and the overlordship of all
client-kings and dynasts west of the Euphrates 'as far as the
Hellespont'; the most westerly dynast known is Cleon in
Mysia, but the phrase may pass. To Cleopatra Selene he
gave as her kingdom the Cyrenaica and Libya. To commemorate the ceremony he struck a coin bearing on one
side his own head and the legend 'Armenia conquered' and
on the other the head of Cleopatra with the legend 'Queen
of kings and of her sons who are kings'; she was therefore
overlord of the whole hierarchy, including Ptolemy Caesar
(p. 103 n. 3). It was a glorious house of cards; whether it
could be solidified might depend on the answer to one pro-
saic question—would the legions fight?

Antony's own position in the new hierarchy of powers
was carefully not defined, for he was filling a double role.
It was necessary, for his Roman supporters and his Roman
troops, that he should remain Marcus Antonius, Roman
magistrate. But to Greeks and Asiatics he was a divine
Hellenistic monarch, Antony who is Dionysus-Osiris, con-
sort of Cleopatra-Isis, queen of Egypt. What was this position of his which could not be defined because of Roman
susceptibilities? It was something which could be inherited;
for he had already (1 January 34) struck the first of the
coins bearing his own head and the head of his elder son
by Fulvia, Marcus Antonius the younger (nicknamed by
Alexandrians Antyllus, little Antony), which shows that
this boy was his destined heir. Again, it was something
which dated an Era, like a king's reign. Documents of the
joint rule of Cleopatra and Ptolemy Caesar in Egypt are
always dated by a single date, the year of her reign; but in
34 there begins to appear in Egyptian papyri a double

dating, the year of Cleopatra equated with another year, and this double dating, found also in Syria, continues till her last year, 22 which is also 7. In the writer's opinion the meaning of this second Era is not now in doubt; it denotes Antony's regnal years,[1] and though the first instance so far known of its use is in August 34, it was reckoned as from his marriage with Cleopatra in 37. Antony then at the time of the Donations was royal and had named his successor. But he was not king of Egypt; Ptolemy Caesar was that. And he was not King of Kings; he was greater than that, for he had given that title away to others, which shows that it was not his design to divide the Roman realm and become king of a Hellenistic kingdom in the eastern half. Only one possibility therefore remains: Antony, supreme ruler of the inhabited world, of the East and of Rome alike—that is, Roman Emperor,[2] with the *oecumene* under his feet, like Caesar. And where he was, there Cleopatra would be beside him, she also supreme ruler of the inhabited world; that is, Roman Empress.[3] The form of oath now attributed to Cleopatra, 'so surely as I shall one day give judgement in the Capitol', only underlined what was already plain.

There was some weakness in Antony which led him to represent intentions as accomplished facts. He had celebrated the conquest of Armenia on a coin two years before it was really conquered; he had given away Parthia when

[1] Of the two alternative views formerly put forward, that which referred this Era to the territorial gifts in Syria in 37 (a curious basis for an Era), became untenable once its use in Egypt was discovered, and that which referred it to Ptolemy Caesar was always impossible as he was joint king with Cleopatra long before 37.

[2] Whether this meant that, if successful, he would have made the whole realm a kingdom on Hellenistic lines, or something more in accord with Roman ideas, cannot be said.

[3] The coin shows that she was overlord of the whole East, including Ptolemy Caesar, king of Egypt; naturally Rome could not be mentioned, but her position must follow from Antony's. She was therefore two separate things, queen of Egypt and Roman Empress.

Parthia had just defeated him; and now he represented himself, or let Cleopatra represent him, as world-ruler because he was going to defeat Octavian. Cleopatra must have known just what the Donations and Antony's Era were worth; but her object was victory, and anything was worth while which might drive Antony forward or influence opinion. She did influence opinion; prophecies of the overthrow and enslavement of Rome by Asia were recalled or renewed, and some Jews foretold that her victory would be the signal for the end of the current world-period, to be followed by the reign of the Messiah. Octavian for his part cared little if Antony gave Roman territory to client-kings—he did it himself later—but Cleopatra as Roman Empress was another matter. It brought the day of battle very close. He had already a larger army and fleet than he could use, but he needed money and public opinion behind him. He understood very well what Cleopatra and Antony meant, and gave himself forthwith to making Rome understand also.

Statements that Cleopatra drove Antony to ruin are not impressive, as he need not have been driven; it would be more important to know her own mind. Was it only ambition with her, or was there something greater behind? Did she share the vision of one of her followers, who saw in her the destined leader of a great uprising of Asia against Rome, of the oppressed against the oppressor, not for vengeance only, but for a better world to follow? What she herself thought we may never discover; we only know the great prophecy of a nameless Greek who foretold that after she had cast Rome down from heaven to earth she would then raise her up again from earth to heaven and inaugurate a golden age in which Asia and Europe should alike share, when war and every other evil thing should quit the earth, and the long feud of East and West should end for ever in their reconciliation and in the reign of justice and love. It was surely no unworthy cause that could give birth to such a vision, or make men, even one man, see in Cleopatra the ruler who should carry out Alexander's dream of a human brotherhood. We know what Augustus was to do, and how Virgil in the *Aeneid* was to interpret it for all time; but if Antony was to be Roman Emperor, and Cleopatra was to be the instrument of Alexander's idea of the reconciliation of East and West, can we say that the ultimate ideals of the two sides were so very far apart after all? What were far apart were the actual possibilities. Past history had shown that if such ideals were ever to be realized, however imperfectly, it could only be done from the West, by a Roman through Romans. No one, Roman or Macedonian, could have done it from or through the East, for he could never have carried Rome with him. In that sense, but perhaps in that sense alone, the common verdict is just, that it was well for the world that Octavian conquered.

4. THE WINNING OF ITALY

But in the West, too, something great had been coming to birth, the consciousness of a united Italy. The statesmanship of two generations before had produced out of civil war a people and made a nation from what had been a city; the labours of the scholars and poets of the Ciceronian age had given that nation a language and a culture. All it now needed was a leader, and that leader would be one who could promise and bring, above all, peace and relief from civil war. But he must give as well the assurance that the hard-won heritage of the Italian people would not be wasted. At the end of 36 Octavian had declared to his rejoicing hearers that the Civil Wars were over; disbandment began immediately, and while some of the veterans were planted in overseas colonies (as the men of the Seventh Legion at Baeterrae in Narbonese Gaul), others were settled on land for which a proper purchase price or compensation could now be offered.[1] But the winter of 36–5 was scarcely past before Octavian was on the move. The suggestion of campaigns against Britain or Dacia can hardly have been seriously intended, save as a proof that the young Caesar had not forgotten any of his father's plans or conquests, for what Italy most needed was security against attack. In the north-west the Alpine Salassi were continually giving trouble, from the north-east the Iapudes and kindred tribes had raided Tergeste and Aquileia unscathed, the colony of Pola had been destroyed about 40, Liburnian pirates infested the Adriatic, and though Pollio had been granted a triumph for his successes against the Parthini (p. 62), the Delmatae still held standards captured from Gabinius in 48. For the proper defence of Italy it was essential to gain the Alps as a boundary and bring the mountain tribes into subjection, whether Salassi in the north or Iapudes in the east, while control of the Ocra pass and of the upper Save meant that Italy would be freed from the inveterate fear of invasion from the east. True, the Dacians were no longer formidable, for the empire of Burebista had split up into four warring kingdoms, but other enemies might try that line of attack. Most important of all was that Octavian must himself preserve his prestige as a soldier and leader, must keep his numerous legions employed and in fighting trim, and must rivet to himself the loyalty and goodwill of the whole Italian people for deliverance from raids. Herein lies the importance of these Illyrian campaigns. Great expectations had been aroused and Octavian elaborated his favourite plan of a complex offensive. The fleet, possibly under Menas, was brought round from South Italy, and

[1] E.g. Capua was recompensed by land in Crete and a new aqueduct.

while Octavian's legates were to advance north-east from Aquileia towards Emona (Ljubljana) and the headwaters of the Save, he himself marched south-east from Tergeste to Senia (Senj) in order to strike across the range of the Kapela and descend by the valley of the Kupa upon the Save.

The region in which the campaigns of the next three years were to be waged corresponds roughly to the western half of the modern state of Yugoslavia, but its condition was then very different from the pleasant valleys of Croatia or the stony uplands of the Karst as they now appear to the traveller. There was little cultivation: thick and tangled forest prevailed, with sparse clearings where the native villagers grew the spelt and millet upon which they relied. The population was a mixture of races with the Illyrians as a substratum: upon this mixture conquering bands of Celts (such as the Taurisci) had imposed themselves, but though their influence was strong—some tribes, for instance, had adopted Celtic weapons and armour—it was not everywhere dominant. Civilization was in an early stage: many of the tribes practised tattooing, some of the Delmatae used to redistribute their land every seven years, and though fortress-towns built of wood crowned hills here and there for shelter and defence in time of war, there were as yet no cities, no common councils and no possibility of united action. In a remarkable passage the historian Dio suddenly breaks into personal reminiscence to record the rigours of the climate and the worthlessness of the land; the tribes are brave fighters and reckless of peril just because they can find nothing in their country which makes life worth living; 'I know,' he adds drily, 'for I have been a governor there myself.'

The programme for the year was carried out with complete success. The fleet, as it sailed northwards, dealt faithfully with the piratical Liburni and the islanders of Melite (Mljet) and Corcyra Nigra (Korčula), killing or enslaving, and received the submission of the tribes on the coast such as the Taulantii. In the north Octavian's *legati* brought over such tribes as the Carni and Taurisci (who became allies and supplied boats for use on the river) and reached Emona. Octavian had chosen the hardest part, the subjugation of the warlike Iapudes amid their rocky and close-timbered valleys; a few strongholds such as Monetium (Brinje) and Avendo (Crkvina) surrendered, but henceforward progress was slower, for the troops had to hack their way through the dense growth that encumbered the valley, while reconnoitring bodies advanced fanwise on the ridges above. An attempted ambush was repulsed and after the capture of Terpo (Gornji Modruš) the army moved on to the capital Metulum where greater resistance was to be encountered.[1] Octavian erected a mound against the wall; the Iapudes, using Roman engines captured in previous campaigns, undermined it. Two more were raised from which four gangways were constructed for the final assault on the wall. But the desperate defenders succeeded in cutting away the supports, and gangway after gangway collapsed till only one remained. The Romans wavered and stood still: the crisis in the assault had come. From the tower whence he had been directing operations, Octavian rushed down, seized a shield and (followed by Agrippa and a few of his bodyguard) advanced across; shamed into courage the soldiers crowded behind, but the weight was too great and the gangway gave way. Though badly injured by the fall, Octavian showed himself at once; his example was enough and the soldiers at the sight of their young general's bravery and danger found themselves again. More

---

[1] The site of Metulum has been hotly disputed; the likeliest appears to be the modern hill of Viničica, not far from Munjava.

gangways were run out, and to this indomitable resolution the doomed town surrendered. Even so there was one last maddened sortie and the wooden walls and houses of Metulum went up in flame. The remainder of the Iapudes now submitted and M. Helvius was left to guard against outbreaks, while the main Roman force headed eastwards for Siscia (Sisak) lying near the confluence of the Save and Kupa. The headmen at first offered hostages and corn, but the sight of this tribute proved too much for the people; they made a furious rush to close the gates and prepared the town to stand a siege. But against such numbers resistance was unavailing, on land and on the rivers the Romans beat off attempts at relief, and in thirty days Siscia fell. In late autumn Octavian returned to Rome, leaving a garrison of over two legions in Siscia under the command of Fufius Geminus; the winter quarters of the others are unknown, but were presumably in Northern Italy.

Rumours of an attack on Siscia forced Octavian to leave Rome before winter was finished; but the garrison had resisted successfully and he turned south into Dalmatia, where Agrippa and other *legati* had been assigned their tasks. He next appeared before Promona (Teplju), a hill-fortress which had been occupied by the Dalmatian leader Versus. Again sheer weight of numbers rather than any tactical skill prevailed and the stronghold, together with the positions on the surrounding ridges, was soon stormed. Marching southwards Octavian passed through the defile in which a few years previously Gabinius had been entrapped and so took all the necessary precautions against surprise. He captured Synodium and began the blockade of Setovia (Sinj) on its impregnable rock, but the season was by now far advanced, a wound he had received in the knee was slow in healing and so, leaving Statilius Taurus in command, he journeyed to Rome to enter upon the consulship for 33 B.C.

His own campaigns had taken him to the Cetina, but his *legati* had pressed even farther, for Appian's mention of the Derbani and of the Docleatae (whose capital appears to have been the modern Duklja, north of Podgorica), shows that at least the northern half of Montenegro was reached and that his forces came very near to the dividing line between Antony and himself, the town of Scodra.

But in the past two years events had been occurring which brought a breach with Antony ominously near (pp. 100 ff.), and it became important to husband his resources and bring the campaigns to a close quickly. Octavian accordingly laid down his consulship on the very first day, just as Antony had done a year previously, and began operations in Dalmatia in early spring. Setovia was forced by famine to surrender, and the Dalmatians at last made their submission, giving 700 hostages, promising to pay tribute and—best of all—yielding up the lost standards of Gabinius. In the west he put a stop to the indecisive campaigns which Antistius Vetus had been waging against the Salassi; Terentius Varro Murena was to settle the account six years later. Apart from this minor check Octavian had every reason to be satisfied with his achievements. The garrisons at Emona and Siscia controlled and guarded a route of great antiquity and barred any invasion from the north-east; his conquests in Dalmatia had secured the eastern Adriatic coast and won him a splendid recruiting-ground for the Roman navies. Illness had prevented him from carrying out the whole of his projects, but he had delivered Italy from a great fear, he had displayed courage and skill as a leader, and he could recite a lengthy list of tribes conquered—Iapudes, Docleatae, Carni, Taurisci, Naresii, Glintidiones, Interfrurini, Oxyaei, Bathiatae, Cambaei, Cinambri, Taulantii, Meromenni—many of them mere names to the Italians as to us, but which he could set in profitable contrast to what he called the in-

activity of Antony. And in the north the consolidation of
the gains made was begun by the planting or refounding
of colonies; to Tergeste (Trieste), which Caesar had made
an Italian colony, he presented new fortifications,[1] Pola
rose again from its ruins as Colonia Pietas Julia, and Emona
became in 34 B.C. Colonia Julia. From their garrisons the
soldiers faced eastwards towards the great river that was
to be the boundary of their Empire, and the linking-up of
communication between Danube and Rhine would tax the
skill of Roman generals for many years to come.

It was not only in military prestige, not only in the
heightened loyalty and improved discipline of his troops
that Octavian had gained: by beautification of Rome
during these years he carried out yet another of his father's
projects, and by a steady revival of pride in the past of Italy
and her religion he filled the people with some of his own
feeling and fostered a national consciousness. The Romans
saw their city adorned by the efforts of Octavian or his
friends and lieutenants. From the booty won in the recent
campaigns he himself rebuilt the Porticus Octavia in which
he deposited the recaptured eagles of Gabinius. In 32 B.C.
he restored the theatre of Pompey at great expense, without
adding his name. L. Aemilius Lepidus Paullus, who had
been on his staff during the Sicilian campaigns, completed
the reconstruction, begun by his father, of that Basilica
Aemilia which Pliny reckoned among the most beautiful
buildings in the world, while Statilius Taurus, after his
triumph 'ex Africa' in 34, began work upon a great stone
amphitheatre in the Campus Martius. Maecenas, who had
been in charge of the city during the Illyrian Wars and entrusted with Octavian's seal, cleared away a hideous stretch
of burial ground on the Esquiline close by the Servian

---

[1] Probably we should date to this period the sending of a colony to Iader
and a grant of citizenship to Senia.

causeway, and transformed it into a spacious park and walks for the populace. Still greater was the energy of Agrippa, who at his own expense assumed in 33 the unwanted office of aedile: by restoring the century-old Aqua Marcia and by raising a new aqueduct, the Aqua Julia, he increased and assured the water-supply of Rome, where hundreds of new basins and fountains, adorned with marble, facilitated distribution: he repaired public buildings, reconditioned the drainage system, relaid streets, and spent money lavishly in providing amenities such as free baths and theatrical performances for the people.

Deeper and nobler was the sentiment that inspired Octavian in rekindling pride in the old Roman religion and institutions and in counteracting foreign practices. Greek cults were not banned for they had been long known to the people, Apollo was his protecting deity, and later, by his initiation, Octavian was to manifest his approval of the 'augusta mysteria' of Athens; but Asiatic, Syrian or Egyptian rites were not to be allowed. In every way men were encouraged to restore the sacred buildings and so reawaken belief. Octavian himself, on the prompting of the aged Atticus, undertook the repair of one of the most hallowed spots in Rome, the temple of Jupiter Feretrius wherein reposed the original *spolia opima* dedicated by Romulus. Cn. Domitius Calvinus, from the spoils of his Spanish campaign, rebuilt the Regia, adorning it with statues provided by Octavian; L. Marcius Philippus restored the temple Herculis Musarum and L. Cornificius took charge of the temple of Diana on the Aventine. Already Horace, shedding his Republicanism, could write of Octavian as one whose care it was to protect 'Italy and the shrines of the gods', and could advise a *parvenu* freedman to make good use of his pile by spending it on decaying temples. Nor were the great priesthoods or the aristocratic families that supplied them forgotten. Octavian

was himself an augur and his reward to the ex-Republican
Messalla Corvinus for his services during the Sicilian War
was the grant of an *extra numerum* place in the college of
augurs. In 33 he was empowered by the Senate to create
new patrician families for the express purpose of filling the
priesthoods; the children of these noble families had been
accustomed to take part in a ceremony (of supposedly great
antiquity) called the Lusus Troiae, and this was celebrated
by young men in 40 and again in 33 B.C. By every possible
means, small and great, material and spiritual, Octavian
was slowly educating Italy to his own faith and giving it
strength for the coming struggle. Significant was the edict
that in the year 33 expelled from Rome astrologers and
fortune-tellers and magicians, those poor Greek or Asiatic
charlatans whose antics Horace used so to enjoy watching:
the time was not so far distant when Octavian as fetial priest
of a united Roman people would demand reparation from
a queen whose more formidable magic menaced the existence of the Roman State.

5. THE BREAK

The agreement reached between Antony and Octavian at
Tarentum was not to last for long. By the winter of 34 B.C.
ominous signs had appeared, yet it is unlikely that the inner
history and exact truth of the important period lying between 37 and 30 will ever be discovered, because the facts
have been obscured and distorted by the propaganda of
both sides, propaganda which has survived (and still defies
complete analysis) in our sources. Some discussion of these
sources is imperative, therefore, at this point, for though
Octavian's ultimate victory did not succeed in obliterating
versions and traditions hostile to himself or favourable
to Antony, the conquering cause naturally pleased the

majority of Augustan historians. In the earliest narrative available, the brief history of Velleius Paterculus, the tone is 'official'; Antony has scarcely a redeeming feature and is wrong almost from start to finish. Still, the fact that both Gaius and Nero could claim descent from Antony must have exercised a restraining influence upon writers, and the ordinary orthodox view is probably represented by Seneca's verdict that 'a great man and of notable ability was turned to foreign ways and un-Roman vices by his love for drink and his equal passion for Cleopatra'. But the fall of the Julio-Claudians made such circumspection unnecessary. Tacitus readily reproduces traditions hostile to Augustus, and in Plutarch, Suetonius, Appian and Dio both sides are to some extent represented. Sometimes the name of an authority is given and the tendency is clear, but usually the strands are more closely interwoven, and it may be suspected that much which now passes for fact is merely an echo from this war of recrimination. On the other hand, merely to reject on suspicion all favourable notices (or alternatively all unfavourable notices) as obvious propaganda leads to impossible reconstructions.

A few instances will show something of the problem. The existence of the society of the 'Inimitables' (p. 51) might be questioned as sheer Caesarian invention were it not confirmed by an inscription; on the other hand the fishing exploit of Antony, which Plutarch sedulously chronicles among his 'Follies', was obviously an attempt by Cleopatra to stir him to war and action. But when Dio, speaking of the banquets that followed the pact of Brundisium, asserts that Octavian entertained 'in a soldierly and Roman fashion' but Antony 'in an Asiatic and Egyptian manner', the cautious will scent a Caesarian writer, especially when in the next sentence Octavian is portrayed as rescuing Antony from the violence of soldiers who were demanding bounties promised after Philippi. And though it is easy to see through such absurdities as the suggestion that Antony was never engaged in the first battle of Philippi and only took part in the pursuit, or the charges made against Octavian's early life—mere stock-in-trade of Italian polemic—other passages do not disclose their origin so readily. What, for example, is to be made of the statement that the triumvirs in the winter of 43–2 seized large sums of money deposited with the Vestal Virgins? Is it simply true? Or is it a convenient fiction utilized afterwards to defend Octavian's extortion of Antony's will (p. 122)? Even though it were possible to track down with absolute certainty the narrative sources that underlie such works as the *Antony* of Plutarch, the *Augustus* of Suetonius, the last three volumes of the *Bella Civilia* of Appian, or books XLIV to L of the History of Dio (for Velleius presents no serious problems), we should be little nearer a solution, for both Asinius Pollio and Livy, to mention the two most favoured candidates, were men of independent judgement and not mere partisans. In such circumstances all that the historian can hope to do is to set forth a probable story based upon close examination of the sources and a sympathetic study of the chief actors.

The pact of Tarentum had included among other clauses two pledges of good faith for speedy fulfilment: Antony was to provide Octavian with a fleet for the Sicilian War, Octavian was to give to Antony in return four legions (pp. 68, 74). Antony fulfilled his part immediately, Octavian did not, and mutual suspicion began again its fatal work. A year and a half elapsed before Octavian gave thought to his pledge, and he went about it in a manner that revealed his resentment over Antony's abandonment of his sister. In the spring of 35 some seventy of Antony's ships were returned to him (which he had neither asked for nor desired) and

Octavia started eastwards with 2000 legionaries and funds. Antony's reply was direct and brutal: he accepted the men and money but bade Octavia come no farther. She must have returned to Rome in the winter of 35–4 and her brother tried to persuade her to leave Antony's house. But he was met by a determination and passion as great as his own; she remained loyally in the house, attending to Antony's interests, receiving his friends and lieutenants and looking after his children. But the facts that Octavian continued his Illyrian campaigns and celebrated the death of Sextus Pompeius by the conferment of fresh honours upon Antony show that, however perturbed inwardly, he was still prepared to preserve the outward semblance of concord.

Antony must have felt differently: Octavian's pledges were worthless, a breach was bound to come; let it come quickly before his armies weakened yet further and before Octavian gained greater strength and favour in Italy. In the winter of 34, therefore, he staged the famous Donations (p. 101), wherein he declared that Cleopatra had been the wife of Julius Caesar and that Ptolemy Caesar (Caesarion) was their acknowledged son. This was a definite step against his fellow triumvir, for it suggested that Octavian was usurping the place and title of another and had no real claim to the allegiance of the soldiers. Such news, reaching Rome in the spring of 33, moved Octavian to angry remonstrance in a letter. He reproached Antony with his ill-treatment of Octavia, his liaison with a foreign queen, and his support of her son. Antony, genuinely surprised, replied that Cleopatra was his wife; if he was married to an 'Egyptian', had not Octavian been ready to offer his daughter Julia to a Dacian? And what of Octavian's own love-affairs? There followed more serious grievances. In accordance with the treaty of Brundisium Antony claimed half the recruits levied in Italy and allotments for his veterans, and asked where the promised legions were; finally he declared that Octavian alone stood in the way of the restoration of the Republic.

To these fair demands Octavian would not reply. Rage at the insult offered to his sister, mingled with his previous mistrust, had made him determined that until Octavia was righted there should be nothing. Instead he suggested sneeringly that Antony should find land for his veterans from his conquests in Parthia and attacked him for his enslavement to the Egyptian queen. This response reached Antony in the autumn while he was still in Armenia (p. 100), and although he made no immediate move in hostilities— for it was not until November that Canidius brought his army to Ephesus—he realized that it was essential for him to reach the Senate and win its approval in the struggle that was bound to come. He addressed to it a dispatch, asking for the ratification of his *acta* (which would include the Donations), and intimating his willingness to lay down the powers of the triumvirate if Octavian would do likewise. From now on began a campaign of vituperation in which partisans of both sides joined, among them Cassius of Parma for Antony and Oppius and Messalla for Octavian. Amid such activities the year 33 closed and with the last day of December the legal term fixed for the second period of the triumvirate expired.

It is especially at this point that we regret the meagreness and inexactitude of our sources. Precedents were few, if any, but it looks as though both surviving members of the triumvirate (or rather the legal-minded among their supporters) could argue with some show of justice that the law merely fixed a day up to which they could hold their powers and that after that only a formal act of abdication on their part or a vote of termination by the original granting body, the Roman People, could end their tenure. Antony certainly kept the title and continued to act as triumvir; Octavian dropped the title, though whether he made use of his powers or not is uncertain. But his tribunician right gave him sacrosanctity, he had the advantage of holding Italy, and he knew he would be consul in 31. The position of a private citizen was not likely to terrify one who, twelve years ago, in equal certainty of the justice of his cause, had appealed to force and raised armies on his own authority, and he must have been aware that whatever illegalities or unconstitutionalities he might commit would be covered (if he emerged victorious) by retrospective legislation—as actually happened in 29 and 28 B.C. It seems likely therefore that while Antony continued to use both the powers and the title of triumvir (for which he had at least an arguable case), Octavian dropped both and relied upon other means, and so could write in his *Res Gestae* that he was a member of the triumvirate for 'ten consecutive years' and no more.

The consuls who entered office on 1 January 32 B.C., C. Sosius and Cn. Domitius Ahenobarbus, were both supporters of Antony, and as Octavian had prudently withdrawn from Rome before the new year came in, it looked as though Antony could at last gain the hearing of the Senate free and unfettered. But there was a difficulty: the consuls did not dare read to the Senate the full contents of the dispatch they had received from their leader, for they guessed how damaging an effect the reiteration of the gifts and titles bestowed upon Cleopatra and her children would have upon public feeling in Rome. So they tried different methods: Sosius, the more fiery of the two, delivered a harangue in praise of Antony and would have made a motion against Octavian had not Nonius Balbus interposed the tribunician veto. Octavian did not delay his answer long, though he surrounded himself with a bodyguard of his friends and soldiers before he took his seat in the Senate-house; there he defended his own acts and attacked gravely both Antony and Sosius, offering to prove by written documents to be produced to the fathers on a fixed day the justice of his cause. None dared utter a word in reply and the meeting dissolved, but before the fixed day arrived both consuls and some four hundred senators had left Rome for the East.

Antony had made no overt move during 33, but with the return of his army from Armenia in November he had finally decided upon war. He and Cleopatra wintered at Ephesus (33–2) amid strenuous preparations, and on the arrival of the consuls he set up a counter-Senate. He removed many works of art from Asia Minor to Alexandria, and gave Cleopatra the library of Pergamum in compensation for the books burnt by Caesar, but it is doubtful if it was ever transferred. The great fleet was mobilized (p. 125); besides her squadron of warships, she supplied half of the 300 transports and probably a large force of rowers. She had undertaken to pay and feed the army and navy, and she started the war-chest with 20,000 talents; this was what she had been working for, and she was ready now to throw in everything she possessed. Antony called up all the client-kings in his sphere except Polemo and Herod, and took an oath of allegiance from them. Polemo was left to guard the Armenian frontier; and though Herod came to Ephesus Cleopatra would not have him with the army, and at her request Antony told him to punish Malchus for withholding her rent. He did defeat Malchus after a hard struggle, but was nearly balked of victory by Cleopatra's general in Coele-Syria, who knew that she only wanted the pair to damage each other. But before leaving Ephesus Herod, who had grasped Antony's situation, tried to take his revenge by telling him that the path to success was to kill Cleopatra and annex Egypt.

This abominable advice was sound, for at Ephesus the radical impossibility of Antony's dual position had become obvious: he could lead Romans against Romans as a Roman, but not as a Hellenistic king, the husband of Cleopatra. There were fierce quarrels between some of his Roman supporters, who wanted the queen sent back to Egypt and kept out of sight and mind, and Cleopatra, who meant to fight in her own war. Antony's officers were of many minds. Some, like Canidius and Turullius, had to follow him whatever he did, as they could expect no mercy from Octavian. Some, like Domitius, were ready to fight for him, but only if they approved of his policy. Some, like the hardened deserters Titius and Dellius, merely meant to be on the winning side at the end. And there were plain honest men who had no wish for war at all; they preferred Antony to Octavian, but their real allegiance was to the Roman State. Cleopatra had the hardest struggle of her life. At one moment Antony ordered her back to Egypt, but she refused to go; the feeling aroused was shown when Canidius, who supported her, said that a woman who was paying and feeding the army and had a better head than most of them could not be sent away, and was at once told that she had bribed him. She strained her influence over Antony to carry her point, and she did carry it once for all, but the trouble was only glossed over, for the cause remained. Antony did his best by declaring that six months after victory he would lay down his powers. In April 32 headquarters were transferred to Samos, and Cleopatra got him into good humour again with the usual banquets and amusements, while the transports were ferrying the army across to Greece; the whole body of Dionysiac artists were gathered in the island, and Antony rewarded them with Priene. In

May they crossed to Athens, and the city gave Cleopatra the honours once given to Octavia. Antony's supporters in Italy sent him a message begging him to send away Cleopatra, but she was strong enough now to have the messenger turned out.

Meanwhile in Rome, though the consuls had left, Octavian had the advantage of holding the capital; he convened what was left of the Senate and read a detailed defence of his position and acts, attacking those of Antony (especially the Donations), and contrasting his own campaigns in Dalmatia and Pannonia with the failures of Antony. For the coming war he must be secure of two things, money and loyalty, the more so since Antony had the support of Egypt's wealth and boasted that gold could win him many friends in Italy. Fresh taxation was imposed, one-quarter of the annual income from all citizens and a capital levy of one-eighth on all freedmen, and a great effort was made to stir up national feeling. Some thirty years ago Pompey had persuaded Naples to pass a resolution urging the recall of Cicero from exile and bidding other municipalities follow suit, and now representatives began to move among the more important towns and municipalities in Italy, with rumours that Antony was drugged and dominated by a foreign sorceress, and suggesting that they should pass votes of confidence in Octavian as leader of Italy. The movement slowly gathered impetus and in May or June Antony took a step which alienated sympathy from him; he sent Octavia formal letters of divorce. For over two years, despite pressure from her brother, she had refused to leave Antony's house; now his messengers expelled her weeping, with the children she was mothering, and the sight and act roused in her brother such a fury of resentment that he did not hesitate to seize an opportunity suddenly placed in his grasp.

At Antony's headquarters the divorce of Octavia was taken to mean that Cleopatra was irresistible; and Plancus and Titius left and went over to Octavian, the first of many desertions. They had been trusted followers; they brought not only information about plans, but also news that Antony had recently drawn up a will (details of which they professed to know), which he had entrusted to the keeping of the Vestal Virgins. Octavian thus learnt that there was in Rome a document which would prove authoritatively to Italy all he wished to prove but had been unable to do owing to Sosius' withholding of Antony's official dispatch to the Senate. The Vestals naturally refused to surrender the will to his request, and he seized it by force, risking the indignation which this act excited. A first glance convinced him that the will did indeed contain what would serve his purpose, and he read it publicly to the Senate. Among other clauses it is said to have included a declaration that Ptolemy Caesar was the true son of Cleopatra and Julius Caesar; but it certainly gave great legacies to Antony's children by Cleopatra, and it directed that he should be buried beside her in Alexandria.

This last provision roused Rome to fury, for it was taken to mean that Antony intended to transfer the capital to Alexandria; he was no longer a Roman, but the tool of the foreign woman. There was a fresh outburst against him, much of it pitiful enough: he had given Cleopatra a Roman bodyguard (they were in fact Galatians), he had acted as gymnasiarch in Alexandria (as he had done without comment in Athens), he walked by her litter or rode with her; the real charge was that he was a traitor to Rome, ready to lead strange foes against her, like a second Pyrrhus. But against Cleopatra was launched one of the most terrible outbursts of hatred in history; no accusation was too vile to be hurled at her, and the charges then made have echoed through the world ever since, and have sometimes been naïvely taken for facts. This accursed Egyptian was a sorceress who had bewitched Antony with drugs, a wanton who had sold herself to his pleasures for power; this one and that one had been her paramours; Caesar's alleged son was the bastard of an unknown father. She was a worshipper of beast-gods, a queen of eunuchs as foul as herself, a drunkard and a harlot; later she was to be called a poisoner, a traitor and a coward.

Some indeed of these jackal-cries needed the assurance of victory before they were voiced at their loudest, but even so the effect of the publication of the will was decisive. A vast body of hitherto uncertain sympathies now swung round definitely to Octavian. By October the discontent that the new taxation had stirred up, culminating in some regions in rioting and arson, had practically subsided and money began to flow in. In the late autumn the whole of Italy, town after town, joined in a solemn *coniuratio*, swearing allegiance to Octavian as its general in a crusade against the menace of the East, a demonstration of the solidarity of that new citizen-body which had been created by the wise statesmanship of two generations before. This oath was taken also by the municipalities in the provinces of the West, Sicily, Sardinia, Africa, and the Gauls and Spains. Fortified by this public vote Octavian could take the final steps: Antony was deprived of his triumviral power and of his right to hold the consulship for 31, and Octavian himself, as fetial priest of the Roman people, before the temple of Bellona, went through the impressive ritual that accompanied the formal proclamation of a *iustum bellum*. But he declared war on Cleopatra alone, not on Antony; partly because he had in 36 announced that the Civil Wars were at an end, but chiefly because opinion would be solid against a foreign enemy. And it corresponded to the facts; it was her war. Nor need we doubt that Octavian believed both in the mandate given him and in himself.

During the turn of the year Antony with his fleet and army was wintering in Greece, while the fleets of Octavian gathered at Brundisium and Tarentum. Though diplomatic interchanges had ceased, publicity and propaganda continued unabated; the legal position of both protagonists was not strong, and no effort that might win support could safely be neglected. Charges and counter-charges now took their final and grossest shape: Antony was ridiculed for posing as Dionysus, Octavian for posing as Apollo; Octavian was a coward; Antony was a madman and a drunkard, a charge which stung him to a personal defence; he abused Octavian's ancestors, and Octavian abused Cleopatra's ministers; political crimes were alleged on both sides, like the Artavasdes matter (p. 99); there were the sexual accusations which for centuries had been a commonplace of propaganda. Unsavoury in itself, this exchange of invective cannot be omitted from the history of the period and must even be stressed, because it had a definite effect upon historical writing of the next century and a half, and through it upon modern works, and it is not too much to say that both the conventional portraits—of Antony as a drunken sot occasionally quitting Cleopatra's embraces for disastrous campaigns, of Octavian as a cowardly runaway, cruel and treacherous in his dealings—are due mainly to this propaganda and are wholly unreal. But they served their purpose.

The beginning of the year 31 greatly strengthened Octavian's constitutional position, for he entered upon his third consulship (which he was to have shared with Antony), having as his colleague M. Valerius Messalla Corvinus. Within a few months everything was in readiness. Maecenas was left in charge of Italy and the capital, all disturbances in the peninsula had been suppressed, the coasts of the Western provinces were protected by naval squadrons, and Cornelius Gallus was dispatched to guard Africa against attack from the East. As soon as the spring sea was fit for navigation, with fleet and transports and accompanied by a large number of senators Octavian crossed the Adriatic.

6. THE ACTIUM CAMPAIGN[1]

Antony's forces reached the coast of the Ionian Sea, his western boundary, about September 32. His fleet, which had picked up the detachments at Cephallenia and Zacynthus, totalled eight squadrons of the line of 60 ships each (one being Cleopatra's, led by her flagship *Antonia*) with their complements of light scouts, normally five to a squadron—over 500 warships; no such fleet had ever yet been seen. He had noted the advantage which Octavian had had over Sextus in the size and weight of his ships, and had outbuilt him. His ships ranged upward to vessels of nine men to the oar, the flagship having ten, while the larger vessels had belts of squared timbers bound with iron to prevent ramming; the crews might number some 125,000–150,000 men. His land army comprised nineteen legions, doubtless the seven of the old army of Macedonia and twelve, now very weak, which had been in Media—about 60,000 to 63,000 men, all Italians and well-seasoned troops; with the light-armed, partly Asiatics, he perhaps had some 70,000–75,000 foot, the latter an outside figure, and perhaps 12,000 horse, partly the remnant of his original cavalry and partly supplied by the client-kings. That Cleopatra undertook to feed an army and navy of these dimensions shows that Egypt was still producing a large surplus of corn (p. 48); but he

[1] For the reconstruction of the battle and the evidence, see Tarn, *Journal of Roman Studies*, XXI (1931), 173.

had formed food depots in Greece and elsewhere. Of his
remaining eleven legions, four under Scarpus were in the
Cyrenaica to watch Octavian's army of Africa under Cornelius Gallus, and the rest were distributed between Alexandria, Syria (under Q. Didius), and the Macedonian
frontier. There was some disaffection in his rear, but of
little account; Sparta under Eurycles, whose father he had
executed, joined Octavian, as did Lappa and Cydonia
in Crete; and during the winter Berytus revolted from
Cleopatra.

The army wintered on a line extending from Corcyra
to Methone in Messenia, the largest force occupying the
Actian peninsula, the southern of the two promontories
flanking the narrow entrance to the Gulf of Ambracia,
which was well fortified. Antony's headquarters were at
Patrae, where Cleopatra struck coins. The life-nerve of the
army was the Egyptian corn-ships, which rounded Cape
Taenarum and came up the Peloponnesian coast. Their
route was guarded by stations at Leucas and elsewhere,
the most southern being Methone, which was commanded
by Bogud, driven from Mauretania by his brother Bocchus
in Octavian's interest. It was a bad position, for it surrendered the *Via Egnatia* and all good land communication
with Macedonia and the East, and was very vulnerable
from the sea; it gives the impression of being chosen by one
whose aim was not to crush his enemy, but to cover Egypt.

To challenge Octavian for the mastery of the world and
then stand on the defensive was strange strategy, and Antony has naturally been blamed for not invading Italy in
the early autumn of 32, while Octavian still had trouble
there. But in fact he had no choice; he could not invade
Italy, not because the season was late or the ports guarded,
but because he could not go either with or without Cleopatra. To take her with him meant that the whole penin-

sula, including his friends, would stand solid against the foreign invader; and she would not let him go without her and perhaps, through Octavia's mediation, come to another accommodation with Octavian, at her expense. As he could not go to Octavian, he must make Octavian come to him; hence the surrender of the *Via Egnatia*, while in winter he withdrew from Corcyra, leaving free the passage to Dyrrhachium. Octavian, he thought, had not the money for a long war and must seek a decision.

But even if we understand why Antony surrendered the initiative, much of the ensuing campaign, as given in our secondary sources, is incomprehensible. Why did Antony not use his great fleet to attack Octavian when crossing? Why was that fleet never used at all till too late? And how came it, when he meant Octavian to cross, that Octavian surprised him—if he *did* surprise him? None of these questions can be answered. We might conjecture that his position and the quarrels in his camp had paralysed his will; that he only wanted to end it somehow, and believed that, given any sort of a land battle, his own generalship must prevail; but it would remain conjecture. Even the details are wrong; Turullius' coins prove that Antony won some victory after which he was hailed *Imperator* for the fourth time, but it cannot be fitted into the extant secondary tradition. Till we come to Antony's final defeat on land, no satisfactory account of the campaign is possible.

Octavian had mobilized 80,000 foot and 12,000 horse, and something over 400 ships; the bulk of his fleet was formed by the large heavy ships which had defeated Sextus, strengthened like Antony's by belts of timber and equipped with catapults for firing Agrippa's *harpax* (see p. 73); his fleet organization is unknown, but he perhaps had more Liburnians (light scouts) than the usual complement. As he possessed far more men and ships than he mobilized, he must have decided that these numbers would suffice—as they did. The land forces he meant to command himself, but the fleet he wisely entrusted to the tried skill of Agrippa. Maecenas he had left in Rome to manage Italy, but he brought most of the Senate with him, except Pollio. Pollio had broken with Antony on his marriage to Cleopatra and was living in Italy, but he refused to fight against his former friend, and Octavian respected his scruples. Octavian crossed very early in 31, while Antony's army was still in winter quarters. Agrippa with half the fleet attacked the Peloponnese, stormed Methone, Bogud being killed, and thus secured a base for his cruisers on the flank of Antony's corn-ships. Under cover of this diversion Octavian with the army landed in Epirus, moved southwards very fast, tried but failed to surprise Antony's fleet from the land (perhaps Antony's victory comes in here), and seized a position on the high ground at Mikalitsi in the northern of the two promontories which enclose the Gulf of Ambracia. Perhaps Antony was not really surprised—witness Cleopatra's unconcern at the capture of Toryne in Epirus; perhaps his fleet was a bait to draw Octavian into a position where he thought he could trap him; but, if so, things did not go according to plan. By the time he had collected his army in the Actian peninsula Octavian had fortified his position and connected it by long walls with the roadstead of Comarus, while Agrippa had stormed Leucas and destroyed the squadron there. From Leucas and Comarus the fleet could now blockade the Ambracian Gulf, so far as galleys could blockade, and prevent the entrance of corn-ships. Agrippa subsequently took Patrae and Corinth and cut off Antony from the Peloponnese.

An unsuccessful sortie of part of Antony's fleet, in which the dynast Tarcondimotus was killed, may show that, as a dynast was on board, Antony was refusing legionaries to the fleet and depending entirely upon his land operations. He crossed from Actium and camped in face of Octavian; then he shipped troops up the Ambracian Gulf, sent his cavalry round it, and attempted by a combined attack to close Octavian in and cut off his water-supply, the weak point of his position. The attack was defeated by the failure of Antony's cavalry, who formed the northern (outer) wing of the encircling force, and two dynasts, Rhoemetalces of Thrace and Deiotarus of Paphlagonia, went over to Octavian. 'I like treason,' said Octavian to Rhoemetalces when he abused Antony, 'but I don't like the traitors.' Antony made an effort to recruit more cavalry and led a second attempt in person; Amyntas, the man he had made, went over to Octavian with his 2000 Galatian horse, and the attempt was completely defeated. Amyntas and the other dynasts may have objected to the alteration of their position under the Donations; but their allegiance was due to Rome, not to a party, and they may merely have believed that Octavian would be victor. Antony recognized the defeat as decisive for the operations on land, and withdrew to Actium.

Instead of besieging Octavian, he was now virtually besieged. The troops and crews who had wintered on the low ground about the Gulf had suffered from disease; his press-gangs provided more rowers, but that did not help the troops. Rations were short; Agrippa had cut him off from Egypt and the Peloponnese, and food had to be brought on men's backs across the mountain paths of Aetolia (Plutarch's grandfather was pressed as a carrier, which helps to explain Plutarch's want of sympathy for Antony), and even this resource might fail, as Octavian had sent detachments eastwards. Officers and dynasts alike were now deserting to Octavian, and Antony's attempt to stop the movement by severity—he executed Iamblichus of Emesa and a Roman senator—only increased it; even Domitius himself, desperately ill, left and went to Octavian to die. Dellius followed; and Antony called a council of war. Canidius wished to abandon the ships, retire into Macedonia, and fight in the open; Cleopatra insisted on using the fleet, and Antony agreed. Octavian learnt his decision from deserters. Cleopatra was right in theory, but it was much too late. At sea, with about 400 ships left—seven squadrons of the line, some under strength—they were on paper still at least as strong as Octavian; what came in question was the legions to man them. In those civil wars in which no principle is at stake, only personal ambition, men easily change sides wholesale; the wars of Alexander's Successors supply many instances, and Antony's troops had seen Lepidus' legions go over. Antony had been beaten on land, and the men, weakened by disease and short rations, disheartened by the desertions of officers, and suspicious that they were really fighting for Cleopatra, were thinking that it was time to end it. Antony knew that all was not well, but believed that the common man would always follow him in battle.

On that coast in summer the wind in the morning normally comes in from the sea, but about mid-day shifts to the north-west and blows with some force. Antony knew that when he came out he would find Octavian's fleet to seaward of him, and he meant to use the wind when it shifted to turn their left and drive them southwards (down wind) away from their camp; were they broken or dispersed, he could starve the camp out. As rowers could not pursue far, he took his sails on board, an unusual course. But in case the battle miscarried he had a second plan, probably known only to Cleopatra and Canidius (certainly Octavian knew nothing of it): they would break through to Egypt with what ships they could, and Canidius would bring the rest of the army back overland. The war-chest was accordingly shipped in secret upon some of Cleopatra's transports, which shows that Antony contemplated the possibility of not returning to his camp; otherwise he would not have risked the money going to the bottom. Probably what actually decided the troops was his order to take the sails; this, to them, obviously meant flight, and they were not going to Egypt to fight for Cleopatra.

The number of Antony's ships shows that he shipped some 35,000–40,000 legionaries,[1] more than half his strength. Octavian shipped about the same force, eight legions and five cohorts; Agrippa commanded this fleet, Octavian being on a Liburnian. After stormy weather it fell calm on 2 September, and Antony's fleet came out and lay on its oars, waiting for the wind to veer; he had six squadrons in line, with Cleopatra's squadron, manned by her own mercenaries and trustworthy, in the rear to stop any preliminary attempts at desertion. He commanded the three squadrons of the right, 170 ships, with himself on the extreme right to lead the turning movement; he had two squadrons on the left and one in the centre, but when the right stretched out to turn Agrippa Cleopatra was probably meant to come up into the gap, completing the centre. Well out at sea Agrippa also lay on his oars, waiting for the wind; he was on his own left, to counter Antony's move and if possible turn him instead and cut him off from his camp. When the wind shifted, Antony and Agrippa raced to turn each other and the ends of their two lines met; here there was fighting, and Antony ultimately lost some ten to fifteen ships, while his flagship was grappled; what Agrippa lost is not recorded. At this point the three squadrons of Antony's centre and left backed water and returned to harbour; the two inner squadrons of his right, unable to follow because of Cleopatra, raised their

[1] The 20,000 of tradition, like the 170 ships, refers only to the right wing, his own command.

oars and surrendered; and Antony was left with nothing but his personal squadron on the extreme right, which was engaged, and Cleopatra's, which was isolated. He signalled Cleopatra to carry out their second plan; she hoisted sail and stood southwards, waiting for him once she was out of enemy reach; Agrippa's right, which may have followed Agrippa, was nowhere near her. Antony could not extricate his flagship; he transferred himself to the first ship of the line which was free and with the rest of his squadron, some forty ships, followed Cleopatra. He boarded her flagship and sat on the prow with his head in his hands, forgetting even her and staring at the sea, but what he saw was not the sea but his ships returning to harbour; he knew now that all was over, for there was scarcely anyone in the world whom he could trust to follow him. From that hour he was a broken man.

Octavian could hardly realize what had happened, and remained at sea all night; but in the evening he had sent a dispatch to Maecenas in Rome with the bare facts, and from this Horace wrote his ninth *Epode*, which records the treachery of Antony's fleet. Next morning, however, he took over the five surrendered squadrons, the '300 ships' of his *Memoirs*. He burnt the larger part, as was Roman practice, and used their bronze beaks to decorate the monument raised where his camp stood and the temple of Divus Julius in Rome. The rest he ultimately stationed at Forum Julii (Fréjus) as one of the Imperial fleets. Canidius tried to get the army away, but though it did not surrender for seven days it was only negotiating terms; finally Canidius had to fly for his life, and went to Antony in Egypt.

Octavian was hailed *Imperator* for the sixth time, and Cicero's son had the satisfaction of reading to the Senate his letter announcing Antony's defeat. Some of Antony's prominent adherents were put to death, but some were spared, including Sosius; his corn was distributed to a hungry Greece and his legions broken up. The veterans from both armies were sent back to Italy and the rest distributed in different places, lest they should mutiny. Octavian sent Agrippa to Italy to aid Maecenas, who during the campaign had had to deal with a plot by Lepidus' son, and himself went to Athens, where he was initiated, and thence to Samos; but the veterans sent to Italy saw themselves excluded from the plunder of Egypt and became so unruly that in January Agrippa urgently begged him to return. At great personal risk from storms he crossed to Brundisium; he distributed what money he had secured or could obtain, and took land for his own troops from communities which had favoured Antony, some of the dispossessed owners being settled at Dyrrhachium and Philippi, and from other communities which became military colonies; but he really tided over the trouble by promising to pay both troops and landowners in full from the treasure of the Ptolemies, and they agreed to wait. He then returned to Asia, with the knowledge that his career and perhaps his life depended on securing that treasure.

7. ALEXANDRIA

Though Antony was broken by the catastrophe of Actium, Cleopatra was not. She sailed into the harbour of Alexandria with head erect and ships garlanded for victory; it gave her the few hours she needed, and she seized and executed all who might have raised a revolution against her. Antony went to Cyrene, but his legions there joined Gallus, and he went on to Alexandria. Cleopatra began to make plans: they might sail to Spain, seize the silver mines, and play Sertorius; they might found a new realm in the Indian seas, beyond reach of Rome. This was feasible enough, and she drew some ships over the isthmus to Heroônpolis; but Malchus joyfully attacked and burnt them. She executed Artavasdes to secure the Median alliance, in case they could defend Egypt. But every plan depended on Antony's co-operation, for she had no thought of abandoning him, and Antony was useless. As men had deserted him, he would desert men, and he was living alone in a house near the shore, playing Timon the misanthrope. The first necessity was to restore him to some sort of sanity, and she tried to do this by the only way she knew of, a fresh round of feasts and amusements, under the shadow of death. He did return to the palace; but as he never attempted to collect his remaining legions and hold the enormously strong line of the Nile, which had so often saved Egypt from invasion, he must have told her that defence was impossible; the troops would merely go over, as the legions at Cyrene had done and as Didius and the Syrian legions soon did. One body of men alone remained pathetically loyal to him: some gladiators training at Cyzicus to make sport for him after his expected victory started for Egypt to help him, but Didius prevented them from passing through Syria and they were destroyed later by Octavian's general Messalla. Antony might have been expected to imitate Cato and Brutus and commit suicide; the sequel shows that he meant to live while Cleopatra lived, perhaps with some vague idea that he might yet be of use to her.

Cleopatra had to decide whether she would defend Egypt by herself; she faced the situation with her usual courage. After her two bids for supreme power she was again what she had been at the start, a client-queen of Rome. That she must lose her throne, if not her life, she knew. But if she fought, her children would fall with her, for the result was certain; if, however, she acted as client-kings did act in such circumstances—as Deiotarus had done and Herod was doing—and put her crown into Octavian's hands, there was a chance that he might follow Roman custom

and give it to one of her sons. She made her decision accordingly, and when Egypt offered to rise for her she forbade it, giving as her reason that she would not inflict
useless suffering on her people; it may well be true, though
her primary reason was her children.

In the summer of 30 Octavian approached Egypt through
Syria, while Gallus occupied Paraetonium. Antony went
there, but merely lost his forty ships. He sent envoys to
Octavian,[1] offering to kill himself and spare him trouble
if that would save Cleopatra; Octavian did not answer. The
stories of Cleopatra's attempted treachery to him (what was
there to betray?) are all demonstrably untrue. Following
her decision, she sent Octavian her sceptre and diadem,
asking him to crown one of her sons. Officially, he ordered
her to disarm. But secretly he assured her that she had
nothing to fear; for she still had one piece to play, the
treasure of the Ptolemies. On the strength of it he had
made many promises in Italy to both veterans and landowners; he still had to face the claims of his victorious army.
If he failed to secure the last great accumulation of wealth
in the world, army, veterans and landowners would all turn
on him in earnest. Cleopatra had built herself a mausoleum,
not yet completed, near the temple of Isis; as Octavian approached, she shut herself up in the upper room with her
two women, Iras and Charmion, while in the lower part
was stored the treasure, gold and jewels, ivory and spices,
heaped round with inflammable matter; should he refuse
the crown to one of her sons, she could light a royal pyre
and bring him to ruin.

On 31 July his advance cavalry reached the suburbs.
Antony could not die without one fight; he fell on them and
scattered them. But that night a sound was heard in the

---

[1] We can neither check nor criticize the story that he first asked for his
life, but it sounds incredible enough; he was no coward.

city not made by man, interpreted as the god Dionysus leaving Antony; and when next day he drew out his forces, his cavalry and Cleopatra's ships (*i.e.* her mercenaries) went over to Octavian, and Antony, returning to the city, heard that Cleopatra was already dead. That was all he had waited for and he stabbed himself, but did not die at once; then he heard that she lived and begged to be taken to her. With much effort the three women drew him in at the upper window of the mausoleum, and Cleopatra mourned him as Briseis had mourned Patroclus, tearing her face and breasts with her hands. He died, as he would have wished to die, in her arms.

That same day, the first of the month afterwards called in commemoration by his name, August, Octavian entered Alexandria. He was not hailed *Imperator* by his troops, as he entered without resistance; but it was publicly recorded in the Fasti that on that day he saved Rome from the most terrible danger, that is, from Cleopatra. He at once sent his friend Proculeius with orders to take her alive. She spoke with Proculeius through a grating and named her terms, the crown for one of her sons; but he saw the window and returned next day with Gallus, and while Gallus held her in talk at the grating he and others climbed in at the window; she tried to stab herself, but was seized, disarmed and carried off to the palace, and Octavian was safe at last; he had the treasure. When it was taken to Rome, the standard rate of interest at once dropped from 12 to 4 per cent, and Octavian was easily able to satisfy all claims of the army and the veterans and pay for all the land he took, though all prices doubled, and, after executing many public works, still distribute a large surplus in bonuses to the people.

He allowed Cleopatra to bury Antony, and he put to death four men: Turullius and Cassius of Parma, Caesar's murderers; Ovinius, a senator, manager of Cleopatra's wool-mill; and Canidius. But he killed the two boys, the young Antony as his father's designated successor, and Ptolemy Caesar (whom his mother had tried to send to the Indian sea for safety) because of his name and parentage;[1] the world must not hold two Caesars. It was the final brutality of a brutal age, and he meant it to be final; if the world was to have peace, he had to make an end of all who might yet trouble it. But there was still Cleopatra. Doubtless Rome expected her death, but he seemingly objected to killing a woman, or even to being thought accessory to her suicide. When on her removal to the palace she began starving herself he stopped her by threatening to kill her children. Yet she must die, both for what she had done and because she knew too much; Cleopatra on some Aegean rock writing her *Memoirs* might have been awkward for the future Augustus. His problem was to induce her to kill herself in such a way that he could not be blamed. Had he really meant to preserve her for his triumph he would have given her a Roman gaoler, with trustworthy women never quitting her; instead, she was left in the palace with her own people in charge of his freedman Epaphroditus, who knew his wishes; if necessary, a freedman could always be disavowed and executed, as Antigonus I had executed the women he employed to murder another Cleopatra.

Cleopatra, her first impulsive attempts at suicide having failed, desired now before dying to be sure that there was no chance of the crown for one of her sons—why had Octavian neither killed nor imprisoned her? Octavian knew her motive through Proculeius; he knew too, as did everyone, that she had declared that she would never be led in his triumph; she was not going to be shamed before the Roman mob, like her sister Arsinoe. On these facts he could work. Which of them sought the interview between them is

[1] That they had been declared of age was not the cause of their deaths.

immaterial; it was necessary to both. It was more than the meeting of two great antagonists; two civilizations, soon to be fused, stood face to face in their persons. What passed was never known but to their two selves; our accounts are merely rhetorical exercises.[1] But Octavian could only say what, if it became known, would not inculpate him, and the sequel shows something of what happened. He told her that he meant to annex Egypt, which removed her last reason for living; and he gave her some vague assurances which he knew that she would see through and would conclude that she *was* to be led in his triumph. Still she did not die, for she wished to die in one particular way; Octavian became impatient, and word reached her, as from a friend, that in three days' time he would take her to Italy. Then she asked his leave to make a libation at Antony's tomb; and over the tomb she prayed—many must have heard—that, as they had not been divided in life, so they might not be divided in death. It was not acting; they could not have done and suffered together what they had done and suffered without her having *some* feeling for him; perhaps she did love him dead whom she had never loved living. One of her people used the occasion to arrange for the asp, and a peasant brought it to the palace in a basket of figs.[2] If the story we have be true—if no snake was seen after her death and yet Octavian at once sent the snake-charmers called Psylli to suck the poison from the wound—then he knew beforehand of the sending of the asp. But he would hardly have given himself away so glaringly, and doubtless the

[1] The story that she made love to him was invented, on well-known lines, to glorify his continence.

[2] The story that she had snakes in the palace belongs to the shameful invention, originating in an anonymous Roman poem, *Carmen de bello Actiaco*, that she tried them on slaves to ascertain what was an easy death, i.e. that she was a coward, the accusation which moved Horace to speak out. The basis of the story may be that criminals in Alexandria were sometimes executed by snake-bite.

story of the Psylli is untrue. On receiving the snake, Cleopatra wrote him a letter, asking to be buried beside Antony; and Epaphroditus, with the palace slaves at command, quitted his post and took the letter himself, the final proof that Octavian intended her to have her opportunity.

Of the manner of her death no doubt should now exist, for it is known why she used an asp; the creature deified whom it struck, for it was the divine minister of the Sun-god, which raised its head on the crown of Egypt to guard the line of Re from harm. Once she was alone she arrayed herself in her royal robes and put the asp to her breast; the Sun-god had saved his daughter from being shamed by her enemies and had taken her to himself. With her died her two women; of how many queens is it written that their handmaids disdained to survive them? So Octavian's men found them when they broke in: Cleopatra dead on her couch of gold, with Iras dead at her feet, and Charmion, half-dead and trembling, trying to adjust the diadem upon her head. One of the men burst out, 'Is this well done, Charmion?' 'Aye,' said she, ''tis very well.'

The ancient world had little pity for the fallen; and it had little for Cleopatra. The hatred which Romans felt for her can be read at large in their literature; but through that literature there runs, too, another feeling, publicly recorded in the Fasti, and if Octavian's propaganda directed the hate, it did not create the fear. Grant all her crimes and her faults; grant that she sometimes fought her warfare with weapons other than those used by men; nevertheless it was the victors themselves who, against their will, raised the monument which still witnesses to the greatness in her. For Rome, who had never condescended to fear any nation or people, did in her time fear two human beings: one was Hannibal, and the other was a woman.

IV

THE TRIUMPH OF OCTAVIAN

I. OCTAVIAN IN THE EAST

Cleopatra died late in August 30 B.C.; she was 39 years old, and had reigned 22 years. Octavian granted her last wish and buried her beside Antony; their tomb is covered by the modern city and will never be disturbed. Before it Octavian set up statues of her brave handmaids, whose names became a proverb for faithfulness unto death. Octavia took her three children and brought them up with her own; the little Sun and Moon walked in Octavian's triumph. The boys are not heard of again, though legend made one of them the ancestor of Zenobia, but the girl was married to Juba II of Mauretania; she made a little Alexandria on the Moroccan coast, but with the murder of her son Ptolemy by Gaius the known line of the Ptolemies ended. Antony's memory was formally obliterated; his name was expunged from the Fasti (though Augustus restored it later), his statues were overthrown, the decrees of honour passed for him by Greek cities were destroyed. The Senate passed a decree that the names Marcus and Antonius should not again be conjoined, though it soon became a dead letter. A village in Lydia continued to honour his memory, and a tribe bearing his name remained at Prusias on the Hypius, and perhaps at Ephesus; otherwise the East retained little trace of him, except for Polemo, who afterwards married his granddaughter Pythodoris and named their elder son, the future priest-king of Olba, Marcus Antonius Polemo, and their daughter, who married Cotys of Thrace, Antonia Tryphaena. But we may perhaps recall, as a problem in heredity, that from him and the gentle Octavia were descended the emperors Gaius and Nero.

Octavian set up many monuments of Actium. He ascribed his success to Apollo of Actium, whose temple he enlarged; the local Actian festival was made quinquennial and equal in honour to the Olympian, as the Alexandrian Ptolemaieia had been; and to Apollo he dedicated his unique 'ten-ship trophy', a ship from each of the classes of Antony's fleet, headed by his flagship. Near where his own camp had stood he founded Nicopolis, a Greek city into which he synoecized most of the cities of Acarnania and Epirus, including Pyrrhus' capital Ambracia, thus degraded to a village by the defeat of the second Pyrrhus. His coins show that he consciously posed as the counterpart of the great Antigonids, who had vanquished the great Ptolemies, Cleopatra's ancestors, as he had vanquished her: Demetrius, who had defeated Ptolemy I at Salamis, and especially Antigonus Gonatas, who had slain Rome's enemy Pyrrhus and had humbled Ptolemy II at Cos. His coin showing Neptune with one foot on the globe recalls Demetrius' Poseidon, while Nicopolis was a copy of Demetrius' unique synoecism of all Magnesia into Demetrias. More important are the coins which show on a ship's prow a copy of the Victory of Samothrace, the statue set up by Antigonus Gonatas to commemorate Cos, while his ten-ship trophy was the nearest he could get to Gonatas' dedication of his flagship *Isthmia* to Apollo, since at Actium he had had no flagship himself. This attitude soon obscured the truth about Actium, for if it were another Cos it must be a great battle, and a great battle it became; the overthrow of the queen who had restored the empire of Ptolemy II must be no less glorious than had been the defeat of her prototype.

From Egypt Octavian travelled back through Syria and Asia Minor, and restored to the cities of Asia most of the works of art carried off by Antony. Before returning to Italy he had to settle the matter of Antony's client-kings, and the settlement he now made may be treated as a whole, without distinguishing what was done before and what after the occupation of Alexandria. The Donations were naturally cancelled, and Cyprus and Cyrene again became Roman provinces; otherwise he made little change in Antony's arrangements. Only two petty dynasts were executed, and that not for favouring Antony but for murder: Adiatorix of Heraclea for a massacre of Romans in his territory, and Alexander of Emesa for inciting Antony to kill his brother Iamblichus; the tyrant Strato, removed from Amisus, was not Antony's man.

In Asia Minor most of the dynasts had come over to Octavian in time. Deiotarus of Paphlagonia, like Rhoemetalces in Thrace, kept his kingdom; Cleon, the one-time brigand chief of Mysia, was made priest-king of Zeus Abrettenios in Aeolis, with Abrettene and Myrene as his domain. The priest-king of Comana Pontica, Lycomedes, although Caesar's man, was dethroned and his office given either to Adiatorix' son Duteutus or to one Medeus, who had revolted against Antony in Mysia. Tarcondimotus of the Amanus had fallen fighting for Antony, and had been succeeded by his son Philopator I; Octavian deposed him and administered the Amanus as part of Cilicia till 20, when he restored Tarcondimotus' line. Of Antony's three important kings, Amyntas had rendered much service to the victor; his kingdom was enlarged by the addition of Isaura and Cilicia Tracheia, which had once been Roman territory but had been given by Antony to Cleopatra; he also took Derbe and Laranda from a local tyrant, Antipater, and till his death was Augustus' right hand. Archelaus remained as he was, though his kingdom was enlarged later. How Polemo made his peace is unknown; but Octavian recognized his value and left him Pontus, and though for a special reason he deprived him of Armenia Minor (p. 144) he gave him as compensation an indefinite right of expansion north-eastwards, of which he was to make full use.

In Greece, beyond giving freedom to Lappa and Cydonia in Crete, who had declared for him before Actium, and founding Nicopolis, Octavian did little, but that little was significant; he rewarded Sparta, his one ally in Greece itself, by enlarging her territory and giving her the conduct of the Actian games, but he also made Eurycles tyrant, thus imitating Antony, who had also set up one city-tyrant, Boëthus, in half-oriental Tarsus.

In Syria, the Phoenician cities regained their freedom, as did Ascalon; Berytus, which had revolted from Cleopatra before Actium (p. 126), received (probably later) an enormous extension of territory. Emesa, vacant by the death of Iamblichus, was administered as part of Roman Syria till 20, when Augustus restored Iamblichus' son. In Chalcis, lately Cleopatra's, Chalcis itself became a free city, but Zenodorus, the son of the former dynast Lysanias, was allowed to rule in Abila and to rent his father's possessions; subsequently he recovered much of the kingdom, but he governed badly and his dominions ultimately passed to Herod. In Judaea, Hyrcanus had foolishly returned from Parthia, and after Actium Herod killed him lest Octavian should make him king. Herod himself had made no submission after Actium, and Octavian sent for him. Like Cleopatra, he removed his diadem and laid it before Octavian, but he was too wise to make excuses; he said that he had been faithful throughout to his benefactor Antony, and if Octavian would try him he would be equally faithful to him. Octavian replaced his diadem with his own hand, restored to him his balsam gardens, and after Cleopatra's death gave him her Galatian bodyguard and all of Palestine except Ascalon which had been hers. The philosopher and historian Nicolaus of Damascus, who had been tutor to Cleopatra's children, now went to Herod and showed with his pen all the zeal of the new convert.

Beyond the Euphrates Octavian did not intend to interfere; he did not even avenge on Artaxes of Armenia his massacre of Roman subjects, beyond detaining his brothers as hostages. Parthia might keep her eagles; when the pretender Tiridates fled to him in 30 he gave him asylum in Syria but refused him support and gave a friendly reception to envoys from King Phraates. But he received Antony's friend, the Median king, with kindness, restored to him his daughter Iotape, and gave him Armenia Minor, which he took from Polemo; for the Mede was now Artaxes' irreconcilable enemy and the right man to guard the frontier.

Apart from the Donations, Antony's more important dispositions west of the Euphrates had thus stood the test, and Octavian's gift or confirmation of territory once Roman to Amyntas, Cleon, and Polemo followed his precedents. It has become a commonplace that Antony's arrangements were bad. Octavian did not think so.

2. WARS IN THE WEST AND THE BALKANS

While men's eyes had been fixed upon the East and what was happening there, the western half of the Empire had been under the guidance of Maecenas; thanks to his tact and vigilance the administration went smoothly, and such an affair as the conspiracy of young Lepidus (p. 133) was easily suppressed. Some minor wars were necessary upon distant frontiers: in spite of Agrippa's campaigns in 39 Gaul was not yet completely settled in the north and west, so Nonius Gallus had to punish an outbreak of the Treveri, while C. Carrinas put down the Morini and drove back the

Suebi who had crossed the Rhine. In 28 B.C. the Aquitanian tribes revolted and apparently invaded the old *Provincia*, and Messalla Corvinus won successes in this western region that earned him a triumph. Britain was left unmolested, for Octavian had more serious problems to deal with, though rumours were abroad that in time he would renew and complete the enterprise of Caesar. In Spain the beginning of the Provincial Era in 38 B.C. may have recorded the hope of peace, but within ten years there was a revolt of the north-western tribes, Cantabri, Vaccaei and Astures. These were crushed by the efficient Statilius Taurus, and from Spain too C. Calvisius Sabinus and Sextus Appuleius made good their claims to triumphs in 28 and 27. Thus Rome saw a succession of such spectacles, for, in addition to Carrinas and Sabinus, L. Autronius triumphed in 28 from Africa, and Messalla celebrated his triumph in the following year. The proceeds of the spoils were used on great public works, both on buildings and on the repairing of roads. Yet few of these campaigns can have roused more than passing interest in a Rome that was busied with greater issues; one, however, demands longer notice, not only on account of the importance of the operations for the defence of the north-eastern frontier, but also because of its political consequences in Rome itself.

When Octavian in 30 B.C. entered upon his fourth consulship he had as his colleague M. Licinius Crassus, who tempered by prudence the ancient Republican tradition of his family: originally attached to Sextus Pompeius, he had joined Antony after Naulochus and then deserted him to serve Octavian before Actium was fought. He was undoubtedly a capable commander, and in the summer of 30 he was dispatched with an army of at least four legions to Macedonia, a province that badly needed a general. Its northern boundaries were always exposed to attack, and though the threat of a united Dacia had faded away (p. 106) there still remained the possibility of raids by the various petty Thracian and Getic chieftains. Graver still was the threat from a migrating Germanic tribe, the Bastarnae, who some thirty years back had appeared in the region of the lower Danube and had inflicted near Istros a serious defeat (involving the loss of some Roman eagles) upon the unlucky C. Antonius. The province offered obvious opportunities to an ambitious governor which Crassus was not slow to seize: so long as the Bastarnae crossed the Danube merely to harry Moesi, Triballi or Dardani, barbarian might kill barbarian, but when their masses broke over the Haemus range and attacked the Denthelete Thracians (in the valley of the Upper Struma), whose blind King Sitas was an ally of the Roman People, he had justification for interference. Early in 29 he drove them out of Sitas' territory towards the northwest and then—taking a leaf out of Caesar's diaries—when they sent him an embassy he made it drunk and so succeeded in entrapping the main body near the river Cebrus.[1] A fearful slaughter followed, in which Crassus had the distinction of killing the Bastarnian king, Deldo, with his own hand. Helped by a Getic chieftain, Roles, he next stormed a strong place occupied by some fugitive Bastarnae. The remainder of the year was spent in savage fighting against various tribes of the Moesi and in repelling attacks from Thracians who were supposed to be friendly. Enough had been done for the year, and he disposed his troops in winter quarters. Octavian, perhaps in the late spring at Corinth, bestowed upon Roles the title of *socius et amicus*; the Senate awarded Crassus the honour of a triumph, and cities such as Athens offered him thanks and dedications. In the next year he

---

[1] The river Cebrus is probably to be identified with the Bulgarian Tzibritza, which flows into the Danube at Cibar, not far east of Lom Palanka.

displayed as great activity: he drove back fresh bands of the Bastarnae who ventured to attack Sitas and his Dentheletae, routed the tribes of the Maedi and Serdi in the north-west, overran nearly all Thrace, helped Roles to counter the attack of a Getic chief, Dapyx, finally capturing the fort to which he had fled for refuge, and, advancing farther north into the realm of a chieftain Zyraxes, he fell on a strong place called Genucla; the fall of this brought with it the recovery of the standards that C. Antonius had lost. Finally he turned westwards and broke the power of the remnants of the Moesi.

The Triumphal Fasti record the celebration of a triumph by Crassus on 4 July 27 B.C. 'ex Thracia et Geteis'. He had shown great energy and rapidity and done much to restore the prestige of the Roman name. In two years he had repulsed the Bastarnae, broken the power of the Getae, and taught the wild tribes of the north-west that Rome would punish those who attacked her allies. Though the boundaries of Macedonia were not advanced and though a province of Moesia was not to be created for some years yet, the frontiers were protected by various client-kingdoms, such as those of Sitas and Roles, and Crassus had increased the power of the kingdom of the Odrysian Thracians by giving it charge of the holy place of Dionysus, which had formerly belonged to the rival tribe of the Bessi: the Greek cities of the Black Sea, now that the dreaded Getic power was humbled, would look to the Romans or their allies as protectors. Crassus had every reason to be satisfied with his achievements and the triumph that he claimed and obtained was well deserved. But his request for another and a rarer honour met with a different fate; to understand why this was we must retrace our steps and see what had been happening in Rome since the year 30.

3. THE FIRST CITIZEN

On 1 January 29 B.C. Octavian entered on his fifth consulship at his winter quarters in Samos, where he was completing his reorganization of the East; that done, he set out for home. He passed through Corinth, and landed in early summer at Brundisium. Ill-health compelled him to rest for some days in Campania, and at Atella Virgil recited the *Georgics* to him. Arrived in Rome he was at length able to celebrate—on 13, 14 and 15 August, amid all the pomp and pageantry that the mind of Rome could devise—a triple triumph for Illyricum, Actium and Egypt. A few days later came the solemn dedication of the temple of Divus Julius and the opening of the Curia Julia. The treasures of Egypt and the spoils of war were used, in accordance with tradition, upon great public works, which were carried out during the ensuing years in the capital and in Italy: the *via Flaminia* was reconditioned as far as Ariminum, eighty-two temples were rebuilt, and on the Palatine the white marble temple of Apollo, Octavian's guardian deity, with its adjoining libraries for Greek and Latin books, could be hurried to completion and was dedicated on 9 October 28 B.C. Apart from the adornment of Rome Octavian was able to put his enormous riches to even more popular uses: towards his triumph the thirty-five tribes of the city had offered him a thousand pounds of gold each as *aurum coronarium* (a usage which had apparently begun with the triumph of L. Antonius in 41). Octavian not only refused to take it, but distributed a handsome gift to the people, and during this and the following year lavished games and shows and made a fourfold distribution of corn. He paid in full all debts that he owed, and forgave all arrears of taxation; a year later all evidence for such arrears was publicly destroyed. Money was plentiful, interest dropped to one-third of the usual rate, impoverished senators were helped by generous presents, and those who had formerly supported Antony were reassured by Octavian's declaration that all incriminating correspondence had been burnt: confidence began slowly to return to a world shaken by twenty years of civil war.

Among the many tasks facing the victor one had already been taken in hand, the reduction of the immense number of legions—some sixty—of which he had become master. In the years immediately following 30 B.C. over one hundred thousand veterans, with full bounties paid, were disbanded and either sent to older foundations or settled in new colonies, in both Italy and the provinces. The sites were selected with care: thus some veterans of Antony were settled at Bononia, a town of which he had been patron and which remained loyal to his memory; Carthage, which had suffered at the hands of Lepidus, was repeopled; twenty-eight colonies in Italy owed their existence to Octavian, and in the provinces such towns as Acci Gemella in Spain, Parium in Mysia, Antioch-by-Pisidia and Berytus in Syria also received veterans as settlers. And these were only the first few of a carefully planned scheme, whereby not only were the claims of the soldiers met but mountainous and wilder regions, such as Western Spain or Pisidia, could be guarded and held in check. Fair payment, as after Naulochus, for the land required was made to the municipalities concerned; the total cost of the settlement over a long period of years ran into hundreds of millions of sesterces. Those soldiers who were retained in service—certainly not more than twenty-eight legions—received gratuities after Octavian's triumph and were employed upon works of public utility, such as cleansing and deepening the canals in Egypt or making levées and embankments to curb the turbulent course of the Adige near Este.

But disbandment was comparatively simple, granted the politic vision of Octavian: it was a question of time and money only, and he now had plenty of both. Far more complicated was the problem of his future position in the State. His victory, like that of Sulla or Caesar before him, had effectively placed the State within his control, and the honours and privileges that Senate and people crowded upon him at the slightest provocation had placed him on an eminence overtopping even theirs. We may agree with Dio that there is no need to dwell upon the decreeing of triumphal arches, images, games and holidays, but two honours of greater significance, belonging to the year 30, must be noticed here. The Senate enacted that in future priests and people should offer prayers for the saviour of the State and that libations should be poured to him at all banquets, an act that set him apart from other men; and the tribunician sacrosanctity granted him six years previously, and which he had had bestowed upon Livia and Octavia (p. 80), was now transformed into something more positive. Octavian was given a power and competence equal to the tribunes in *auxilii latio* (and presumably in *coercitio* and *intercessio*), and indeed more than equal, since his *auxilii latio* was extended to one mile beyond the city boundary and he received some form of appellate jurisdiction. The full possibilities and significance of this *tribunicia potestas* were only to become apparent later; here we need only admire the sure instinct that Octavian displayed in this new constitutional expedient.

The tribunician board had been the only body to offer effective opposition to Caesar; as early as 44 Octavian may have sought to be elected tribune (p. 14), and as late as 32 it was the veto of Nonius Balbus that saved him from the attack of the Antonian consuls; now at one stroke he placed himself at the head, as it were, of the tribunes and beyond their reach,[1] and also established the principle that the powers of an office could be separated from the title and conferred upon a person not holding that office, just as two years later censorial power was conferred on two men who were not censors.

On 1 January 29 B.C. the Senate confirmed all Octavian's *acta*, and a few weeks later the news of the successful negotiations with Parthia produced a fresh crop of decrees: the temple of Janus was to be closed and the long-neglected ceremony of the Augurium Salutis revived. The meaning of these resolutions was unmistakable. Octavian had saved the Roman State, hence the dedication to him by Senate and People in this year of an arch RE PUBLICA CONSERVATA; his final victory had put an end to all wars at home and abroad, an end which was symbolized by the closing of Janus; lastly, Octavian was himself an augur so that it was fitting that the college of augurs should ordain prayers for salvation for the State in the year in which its saviour returned to Italy. There were not lacking other marks of his pre-eminence: the Senate voted that his name should be included in the litany of the Salii, the consul Valerius Potitus offered public sacrifices and vows on his behalf—a thing unprecedented—and at the triumph in August the magistrates and officials instead of guiding the *triumphator* into the city, as heretofore, followed behind his chariot. The title of *Imperator* which Octavian (originally perhaps in answer to Sextus Pompeius' arrogation of the title *Magnus* to himself) had been employing unofficially for some ten years he now assumed officially. At the request of the Senate he was empowered not only to add as many members as he pleased to the priestly colleges, but also (under a Lex Saenia late in 30 B.C.) to create at his own choice new

---

[1] In 29 he prevented a tribune elect, Q. Statilius, from proceeding to office, by what means we are not told.

patrician families—for the ranks of these had been terribly thinned by years of civil war and proscriptions—and so aid in keeping alive the ceremonies and rites upon which the well-being of Rome depended.

Yet this accumulation of honours, which might have glutted the vanity of a Pompey, was a danger-signal to the more sober mind of Octavian, for he could not but remember that it was up this same dizzy path that Caesar had been led, to fall more fatally. However absolute his power—and it was no untruth when he claimed later that the State had been in his hand—it was essential to its continuance that he should not shock Republican tradition or sentiment; there must be nothing to point to a second Ides of March. On the contrary, all appearances indicated a gradual return to stability and the customary forms of government. In the year 28 he entered upon his sixth consulship, with the faithful Agrippa as his colleague; for the first time in twenty years two consuls held office together in the capital for the full twelve months, and Octavian shared the twenty-four lictors that accompanied him with his colleague so that each possessed the traditional twelve. At the end of his term of office he could take the customary oath that he had preserved the laws, a claim that was echoed by coins of the year with the legend LIBERTAT I S P. R. VINDEX. With Agrippa he held a census of the whole people (a ceremony neglected since 70 B.C.) and carried out a revision of the list of the Senate, which had been swollen to an unwieldy number; it was now purged of its less worthy members, reduced from a body of 1000 to some 800, and Octavian himself was enrolled as Princeps Senatus.[1]

---

[1] In the previous year Octavian (perhaps through a *Senatus consultum*), in order to secure full attendances, forbade senators to leave Italy without his permission.

Yet while a return to constitutional correctness was fore-shadowed by these proceedings there were signs of innovation. When Octavian and Agrippa carried out the census they had not been elected censors, nor did they act by virtue of any power originally inherent in the consulship; they received something new, a special grant of *censoria potestas*—that is the conferment of the powers of the censorship upon persons not holding the office—and this development of the conception of *potestas* was soon to be put to important uses. Whereas formerly the *lectio Senatus* had always preceded the holding of a census, on this occasion it was performed while the census was already in progress. And though Octavian was nominally consul, coupled with a colleague of equal authority, the honours and privileges heaped upon him and the enormous prestige that he enjoyed proclaimed him something far higher than the ordinary Republican magistrate. The praenomen of *Imperator* was a perpetual reminder of the victories he had won, his tenure of the augurate and other priesthoods pointed to him as upholder and honourer of the old Roman religion, and the inclusion of his name in the Salian litany suggested something more than mortal. Like Romulus he had been favoured by the sight of twelve vultures when taking his first auspices, like Romulus he had chosen and created patrician families, the very stars that presided over his birth—so it began to be rumoured—were the same as those that had heralded Romulus' greatness; he was the heaven-sent restorer and second founder of Rome. 'Quis populo Romano obtulit hunc divinum adulescentem deus?' Though he was nominally a consul and no more, in reality the State was his to remould as he wished.

The need for some remoulding was obvious from the tragical history of the past hundred years. For such a task Octavian had the advantage of a prestige greater than all his predecessors save only Caesar, and unlike Caesar he had now no active opposition to fear. Civil war and proscription had decimated the older Optimate families, the rest of Italy yearned for peace and stability, it mattered little under what name. But that was the negative side merely: no man can win and retain supreme power in a nation by the simple slaughtering of all opponents; he must be able to convince a majority of supporters that he has something definite and acceptable to offer them. This is what Octavian had done. Though his adoption by Caesar linked him to the noblest and oldest families in Rome, he had none of the narrowness that marred many a Roman aristocrat. By birth, upbringing and sentiment he was Italian, and had appealed to the deepest instincts and traditions of the population of Italy, which had stood steadfast for Caesar. That had brought him first the co-operation and fidelity of a band of able and devoted friends, and finally the overwhelming response of the *coniuratio totius Italiae*. But the very success of his appeal and the conscious sentiment it had aroused fettered him and circumscribed the area of political conceptions in which he could move; powerful though he might be he could not impose his will except in so far as his will interpreted the desires of the Italian people. In consequence it might be not unfairly urged against him that he was compelled to adopt a programme that was too definitely 'Western' in its outlook, and which placed Italy and things Italian too much in the centre of the stage.

For the time being, however, he had made no public decision as to the future form of the government, content with holding the consulship yearly and with the prestige and powers he possessed. How long this might have continued cannot be said, but an incident arising out of the victorious campaigns of Crassus almost certainly forced him to declare himself and accelerated a settlement. For his prowess in killing the Bastarnian king Deldo Crassus had claimed the right to deposit *spolia opima* in the temple of Jupiter Feretrius on the Capitol, the restoration of which had been begun by Octavian in 32 B.C. It was an honour that tradition granted to three Romans only, Romulus, A. Cornelius Cossus and M. Claudius Marcellus, the hero of Clastidium, for though an ordinary soldier might be awarded *spolia opima* for killing an enemy leader the privilege of dedicating the spoils in the temple of Feretrius had been by custom reserved for those generals who were fighting under their own auspices. But the awkwardness for Octavian of such a claim at such a moment needs no underlining; the new Romulus could ill afford to have a rival in military glory. To the objection, however, that the victory had been gained not under Crassus' auspices but under Octavian's, Crassus was able to find an answer in the precedent of Cossus, who according to accepted tradition had been simply a *tribunus militum* and no independent commander when he was granted the privilege. It was therefore fortunate for Octavian that during the restoration of the temple of Feretrius the actual spoils dedicated by Cossus were discovered, together with an inscription showing that at the time he was consul and not *tribunus militum*, and this new evidence was enough to bar Crassus' claim. Though he was allowed to celebrate a well-merited triumph on 4 July 27 B.C., the title of *Imperator* was withheld; in the ensuing years his services were no longer required.

But this occurrence and the negotiations in connection with it revealed clearly that some form of settlement was pressing and that it was essential that in any such settlement the legions and their commanders (or the greater part of them) should be under the acknowledged control of Octavian. In the next year, 27 B.C., he was to be consul for the seventh time, with Agrippa again as his colleague. There is some slight evidence that the work of reform had already been begun and that laws encouraging marriage and penalizing celibacy, forerunners in fact of his later social legislation, were passed in this year, only to meet with such opposition that they had to be rescinded. But their date and content, if indeed they happened, cannot be determined with any certainty, whereas Dio does record for us an important decree that met with universal favour: 'Since Octavian had given many illegal and unjust orders during the strife of the civil wars, and especially during the triumvirate with Antony and Lepidus, he annulled all these in one edict, fixing his sixth consulship as the limit of their validity.' Details of this comprehensive measure are unfortunately lacking; it is possible that some grants already made had to be iterated in order to secure their validity, and we can safely infer that all disabilities attaching to the children of the proscribed and similar inequities were removed. But its general intent and effect cannot be doubtful; it was a fresh step towards that restoration of constitutional government that Octavian had promised after the victory at Naulochus. In sixteen years he had avenged his father's death and attained to more than his honours, he had surmounted all opposition and made himself master of the Mediterranean world. If he was to bring lasting peace, if he was to be called (as he longed to be called) 'the creator of the best constitution', he must attack soon a problem that had baffled Sulla and Caesar. The wars were over; the period of constructive statesmanship could begin.

BIBLIOGRAPHY

Full bibliographies can be found in volume x of the *Cambridge Ancient History*. A selection only is printed here. It is divided into three parts: the authors' own survey of the sources; works by the authors which support their text; other works. The bibliography does not include any books which have been published since 1934 and were therefore not available to the authors when this book was written.

I. SOURCES

The sources for the western half of the Empire in the period covered by this book (44–27 B.C.) diminish both in quantity and in quality the farther we get from 44. At the beginning there is first-rate contemporary material, Cicero's own *Letters* and *Philippics* and (embodied in the *ad familiares*) letters to and from the leading generals of the time, Lepidus, Pollio, Plancus, Cornificius, and Brutus and Cassius. When these cease in the summer of 43 there remain only secondary sources: the *Periochae* of Livy show roughly the view that he took, but little more; Velleius Paterculus presents a short 'official' narrative making Antony the villain of the piece; both writers probably drew a good deal of their material from Augustus' own *Memoirs*. These are lost, but the *Res Gestae*, in its curt references to this period, represents Augustus' view and occasionally gives information otherwise lacking, as, for example, the *coniuratio Italiae*. The later parts of Plutarch's *Lives* of Cicero and Brutus are relevant but add little of real value; his *Life* of Antony however is useful. Suetonius' *Divus Augustus* offers important information, the more so as the authorities are often cited by name, but lacks precision especially in chronology.

In the main any connected narrative must depend on the later compilations of Appian and Dio Cassius. Appian's *Civil Wars*, II, 116 to V, 145 (based mainly on Asinius Pollio, but also on other contemporaries such as Messalla and Augustus himself), are extremely valuable in their facts and figures, but unfortunately end at 35 B.C. Dio is not at his best: books XLV, 20 to LIII, 3 provide a convenient framework but are full of rhetoric and motivation of his own and of the propaganda of both sides.

The contemporary material for Antony and Cleopatra (i.e. the Eastern side of things) during the years 42–30 B.C. consists of a few papyri and inscriptions, including the Fasti; coins, especially those of Antony and Octavian; some fragments; and several poems, the most important being Horace, *Epode* IX and *Odes* I, 37, Virgil, *Eclogue* IV, and *Oracula Sibyllina* III, 350–61, 367–80. Of the secondary sources the best is Book V of Appian's *Bella Civilia*, which stops with 35; the excellent military details, and the comparative impartiality towards Antony, seem to the present writer to show that its main source can only be Pollio. Plutarch's *Life* of Antony is notable among his *Lives* in being unsympathetic towards its subject—towards Antony throughout, towards Cleopatra down to chapter 77, where he begins to use Olympus; apart from his own family traditions his other sources are unknown, except that the invasion of Parthia is from Dellius and parts of Actium from an eyewitness on Octavian's fleet who had deserted from Antony. Dio Cassius XLVIII–LI, 19, partially represents Livy (also represented by his usual epitomizers), and thus in part goes back ultimately, with whatever modifications, to Augustus' *Memoirs*; but his value for Antony and Cleopatra is small. Josephus, *Antiquitates* XIV [12], 301–XV [7], 218, *Bellum Judaicum* I [12], 242–[20], 397, has preserved some valuable facts, but his chronology is most confused. For Parthia, beside the classical writers, the only materials are coins, the Susa poems, of uncertain interpretation, and a parchment from Doura.

The two main literary authorities for the Illyrian Wars are Appian, *Illyrica* 13 and 15–28 (parts of which may be derived from Augustus' own *Memoirs*), and Dio XLIX, 34, 2 and 35–8.

2. WORKS BY THE AUTHORS

(*a*) M. P. Charlesworth:
'The Fear of the Orient in the Roman Empire', *Cambridge Historical Journal*, II (1926), p. 9.
'Some Fragments of the Propaganda of Mark Antony', *Classical Quarterly*, XXVII (1933), p. 172.
[Cf. *The Virtues of a Roman Emperor: Propaganda and the Creation of Belief*, British Academy, Raleigh Lecture, London, 1937.]

(*b*) W. W. Tarn:
'The Battle of Actium', *Journal of Roman Studies*, XXI (1931), p. 173.
[Cf. 'Actium: a note', *ibid.* XXVIII (1938), p. 165.]
'Antony's Legions', *Classical Quarterly*, XXVI (1932), p. 75.
'Alexander Helios and the Golden Age', *Journal of Roman Studies*, XXII (1932), p. 135.
Tiridates II and the Young Phraates. Mélanges Glotz. Paris, 1932, p. 831.

3. OTHER WORKS

Bevan, E. R. *A History of Egypt under the Ptolemaic Dynasty.* London, 1927.
Craven, L. *Antony's Oriental Policy until the Defeat of the Parthian Expedition.* Univ. of Missouri Studies, III, 1920, no. 2.
Hadas, M. *Sextus Pompey.* New York, 1930.

Hill, G. F. *Historical Roman Coins*. London, 1909, nos. 81–4.

Holmes, T. Rice. *The Architect of the Roman Empire*. Oxford. Vol. I, 1928; vol. II (27 B.C.–A.D. 14), 1931.

Macurdy, G. H. *Hellenistic Queens*. Baltimore–London, 1932.

Marsh, F. B. *The Founding of the Roman Empire*. Ed. 2. Oxford, 1927.

Mattingly, H. *Roman Coins*. London, 1928, pp. 83–5.

Mommsen, Th. *The Provinces of the Roman Empire from Caesar to Diocletian*. (English translation by W. P. Dickson in 1886, reprinted with corrections in 1909.) London, 1909.

Reinhold, M. *Marcus Agrippa. A Biography*. Geneva–New York, 1933.

Rostovtzeff, M. *The Social and Economic History of the Roman Empire*. Oxford, 1926. Ed. 2. [New ed. 1957.]

Rostovtzeff, M. *A History of the Ancient World*. Vol. II, *Rome*. Oxford, 1927. [Paperback ed., 1960.]

Sands, P. C. *The Client Princes of the Roman Empire under the Republic*. Cambridge, 1908. (See review by J. G. C. Anderson in *Journal of Hellenic Studies*, xxx (1910), p. 181.)

Scott, K. *The Political Propaganda of 44–30 B.C.* Mem. Amer. Acad. Rome, vol. XI (1933), p. 1.

Shuckburgh, E. S. *Augustus: The Life and Times of the Founder of the Roman Empire* (63 B.C.–A.D. 14). London, 1903.

Wells, J. and Barrow, R. H. *A Short History of the Roman Empire to the Death of Marcus Aurelius*. London, 1931.

INDEX

Where the mention of a name does not record a fact of importance, the name is usually omitted. The following abbreviations are used: A. = Antony; C. = Cleopatra; O. = Octavian.